"An incredibl..." ...f THNK,
School of Creative Leadership

"Neil Pavitt writes the user's guide your brain never came with. Full of fascinating anecdotes and mind boggling research from across the world, he shows how our brains are fallible, gullible, malleable and, ultimately, incredible. We just need to learn how to use them. This book shows you how."
Ian Gilbert, Founder of Independent Thinking

"Cover-to-cover packed with wisdom, wrapped in fun and entertaining anecdotes. There are over 40 golden nuggets in this book, all easy to mine and own and apply to everyday life. A very rare thing indeed – a useful book for people who want to upgrade their brainpower."
Marc Lewis, Dean at The School Of Communication Arts

"This book is a must-read for anyone who wants to discover the full extent of their creative potential. It's jam-packed full of simple yet highly effective strategies and techniques that will 'sculpt' your brain and significantly impact the way you think and how you create – now and forever!"
Gabriella Goddard, Founder and CEO of Brainsparker App

"Neil Pavitt has a rare talent for making what could be difficult subjects accessible and simple to understand. His new book gives you the tools to train your brain and think smarter. Fascinating stuff. I learnt a lot."
Peter Freedman, Director of Thinking at Think Inc

"Neil Pavitt transforms scientific discoveries about how your brain works into wondrous stories that will fire up your imagination. You will form new neural pathways just by reading this book...and if you try his simple brainhacks you will develop the skills to optimize your brain."
Linda Naiman, Founder of Creativity At Work

Brainhack

Tips and tricks to unleash your brain's full potential

Neil Pavitt

CAPSTONE
A Wiley Brand

This edition first published 2016

© 2016 Neil Pavitt

Registered office

John Wiley and Sons Ltd, The Atrium, Southern Gate, Chichester, West Sussex, PO19 8SQ, United Kingdom

For details of our global editorial offices, for customer services and for information about how to apply for permission to reuse the copyright material in this book please see our website at www.wiley.com.

Wiley publishes in a variety of print and electronic formats and by print-on-demand. Some material included with standard print versions of this book may not be included in e-books or in print-on-demand. If this book refers to media such as a CD or DVD that is not included in the version you purchased, you may download this material at booksupport.wiley.com. For more information about Wiley products, visit www.wiley.com.

Library of Congress Cataloging-in-Publication Data

Names: Pavitt, Neil, author.
    Title: Brainhack : tips and tricks to unleash your brain's full potential/Neil Pavitt.
    Description: Chichester, West Sussex, United Kingdom : John Wiley & Sons, Inc., 2016. | Includes bibliographical references.
    Identifiers: LCCN 2015038324 | ISBN 9780857086426 (pbk.)
    Subjects: LCSH: Psychology, Applied. | Brain. | Cognition. | Mental efficiency.
    Classification: LCC BF636 .P386 2016 | DDC 153.4—dc23
    LC record available at http://lccn.loc.gov/2015038324

A catalogue record for this book is available from the British Library.

ISBN 978-0-857-08642-6 (paperback) ISBN 978-0-857-08644-0 (ebk) ISBN 978-0-857-08643-3 (ebk)

Cover design: Wiley
Cover image: © gst/Shutterstock

Internal pages designed by Andy Prior Design Ltd

Set in 9/12pt Myriad Pro by Aptara, New Delhi, India

Printed in Great Britain by TJ International Ltd, Padstow, Cornwall, UK

For Kalya and Harry

CONTENTS

PART

THINKING SMARTER

PART 2

GETTING STARTED

66 **There are billions of neurons in our brains, but what are neurons? Just cells. The brain has no knowledge until connections are made between neurons. All that we know, all that we are, comes from the way our neurons are connected. 99**

Tim Berners-Lee

INTRODUCTION

Are you ready to become a hacker?

Probably the first thought that comes to most people's minds when they hear the term "hacker", is of someone who seeks and exploits flaws in a computer system or network.

In a way, that's what this book aims to help you to do. It's just that the network you're trying to find a flaw in, is your own brain.

Amazingly 95% of your brain's day-to-day activity is unconscious. One hundred billion neurons, one hundred trillion connections and we're only in control of a tiny 5% of it.

The forty-five brainhacks in this book aren't going to suddenly give you control over huge swathes of your unconscious. That would be a nightmare. It's unconscious for a reason; the last thing you want, is to constantly have to think about putting one foot in front of the other every time you go for a walk.

But what these brainhacks will do, is open a window onto some of the activities we do unconsciously and reveal some of the biases our conscious mind has. The aim of this is to help you become more productive, more creative and help you see more clearly why you do what you do.

The purpose of the book is not to give you deep insights into how the brain works, but to give you practical tips and techniques that you can actually benefit from.

All the brainhacks in this book can be read independently, so if you do want to dip in and out, that's fine. However, I have tried to give them an order, so they work better if you read them chronologically.

The first two sections cover general ways to make your brain work better for you, as well as how to use your time more wisely and be more productive. The last three are about how to be more focused in your thinking, how to solve problems better and create more innovative ideas.

One of the most important things to remember is how flexible the brain is. You really can change how you think and act. There aren't analytic people, creative people, focused thinkers and dreamers. These are qualities a person might have, but they're not set in stone.

Our brains actually physically change shape depending on how we use them. It's called neuroplasticity.

The most famous example of this is with London taxi drivers. They have to spend years learning the streets of London before they get their badge. The effect of this is that the area in the brain that deals with spatial awareness, the hippocampus, is larger in London taxi drivers. However, once they retire, their hippocampus returns to its normal size.

Now think of people with dyslexia. They might have learning difficulties, but they certainly don't have achieving difficulties.

Einstein, Beethoven, Steve Jobs, J.F. Kennedy, Leonardo Da Vinci, Agatha Christie, Walt Disney, Picasso, Mozart, Jamie Oliver, Cath Kidston, Steven Spielberg, Jennifer Aniston, Richard Branson and Winston Churchill are/were all dyslexics. Also people with dyslexia are also four times more likely than the rest of the population to become self-made millionaires.

Dyslexics' minds have to adapt to get over their difficulties with language, by learning to become more adept at thinking visually and seeing the bigger picture.

Santiago Ramón y Cajal, one of the founders of neuroscience said, "Any man could, if he were so inclined, be the sculptor of his own brain."

And that's what I aim to do with these brainhacks. Give you the tools to sculpt your brain, to help you to unleash its full potential.

And it really is about sculpting. At two years of age, we have the most synapses (the connectors between neurons) that we'll ever have. By the time we've reached seventy, that number is likely to have halved. In between then, in the same way a gardener prunes a shrub, our brains are shaped by how we use them.

I really hope you find these brainhacks interesting and useful, and hopefully they'll lead to you doing some neural topiary of your own.

66 **In the same way a gardener prunes a shrub, how we use our brain shapes it. 99**

PART I

Thinking Smarter

General ways to make your brain work better for you

1 Make a Done List

> "What you get by achieving your goals is not as important as what you become by achieving your goals."
> *Zig Ziglar*

Before you read this, I want you to leaf through your work diary.

Is there anything inspiring in there? Were you impressed by how much you've achieved?

I know when I look through old work diaries, all I find are lists of meetings and to-do lists.

Even on your phone or laptop, there are endless productivity apps enticing you in to make to-do lists in new and different ways.

The trouble with to-do lists, is I don't think they make us any more productive. I don't think they excite and stimulate our minds to want to get things done.

Usually we don't finish them anyway, which immediately has a negative effect.

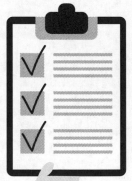

Now I'm not saying we should do away with to-do lists. We all need reminders of what we've got to do. What I'm saying is, they serve a useful purpose of reminding us of things we need to do, but they're not actually going to make us more productive.

What you need is a done list. Seeing what you've actually achieved will spur you on. Of course, you may look back and think how little you have achieved, but hopefully this will also spur you on even more.

One of the dangers of to-do lists is we think we're being productive because we're ticking things off a list. But how many of those things you're ticking off are things you truly value? The benefit of a done list, is you only put things on it that are of value to you.

So how do you decide what is of value and is worthy of putting on your list? Well, for starters you don't want to put everything on it, for example, "Called Debra in accounts" or "Had meeting with marketing", otherwise it just becomes a completed to-do list.

A good rule of thumb, is only put things on it that at the end of the year you'd look back at and be proud of.

To-do lists are about goals, a done list is about achievements.

One of the big differences of a done list, as opposed to a to-do list, is the positive effect it has on your brain.

A to-do list gets the things you have to do out of your head and onto paper. It unclutters your brain. The trouble is, how often do you complete the list? I find I do half of it and then the rest gets transferred to the next day's list.

A long to-do list means: "we've got a lot to do" – it doesn't mean we do a lot.

> ❝ **To-do lists are about goals, a done list is about achievements.** ❞

Unconsciously it changes from a to-do list into a "what you haven't done list" and creates more stress and anxiety.

A done list of things you have achieved creates positive associations and creates new connections in your brain making you feel more positive about yourself.

Of course the danger is to think that you feel you can only put big achievements on there, but this couldn't be further from the truth. If this is the year that you decide to run a marathon, don't just make an entry on the actual day you ran a marathon, put in an entry for how long you ran on each day you trained leading up to it.

Don't Break the Chain

What's important is that you have achievable goals that you stick to. If you make your targets too hard, you either won't achieve them and feel you've failed, or you'll put them off for a day and then another day and before you know it, you've given up on the task completely.

Just try to do a little bit every day

When comic hopeful Brad Isaac asked Jerry Seinfeld[1] if he had any advice he replied that the way to be a better comic was to create better jokes and the way to create better jokes was to write every day. How he made sure he kept to this was a done list in the form of a wall calendar.

He got a big calendar that had a whole year on it, and hung it on the wall next to his desk. Every day he completed his task of writing he'd put a big red X over that day.

"After a few days you'll have a chain. Just keep at it and the chain will grow longer every day. You'll like seeing that chain, especially when you get a few weeks under your belt. Your only job next is to not break the chain," said Seinfeld, emphasizing "Don't break the chain."

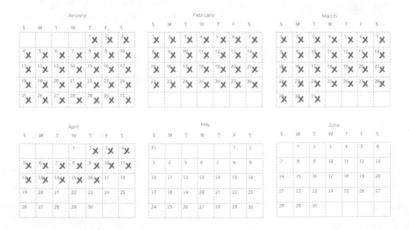

If you're building a house, you can stand back at the end of each day and admire how much you've built that day. But the trouble with a lot of our tasks on a day-to-day basis is that there's no physical proof of what we've done. That's the great thing with a done list, as in the example of Seinfeld's calendar, you can stand back and be proud of what you've achieved.

The thing with a done list is it can be about anything. What's important is that it's something of value to you. It could be steps towards starting your own business, it could be about how much weight you've lost, how much time you've spent reading a book; if you're some high flying businessman or woman it could be about how much quality time you managed to spend with your family. Like I say, it can be about anything, but it has to be something that you value.

What I'd recommend is having a done list calendar like Jerry Seinfeld for the one task you want to push yourself to work on everyday. But as well as this I'd recommend you start a done list diary.

Don't just get some cheap office diary, get a nice diary like a Moleskine; something you'll treasure. After all, it holds your achievements for the year, so it should be something a little bit special. Try to review your day's achievements and make your entry in your done list diary at the same time every day.

The more you can make a habit of it, the more likely you are to keep to it. The more of a habit you make of it, the more you start to create more engrained pathways in the brain to make it harder to stop. Seinfeld's motto "Don't break the chain" has the obvious visual reminder of a calendar on the wall, but at the same time it is creating an unconscious habit.

They say "history will be the judge". Now your history will be there for you to judge.

66 **The more you can make a habit of it, the more likely you are to keep to it. 99**

2 Change Your Memories

"Remembrance of things past is not necessarily the remembrance of things as they were."
Marcel Proust

Most people would like to have a better memory, but you'll already find lots of tips and techniques online to help you with that. What this hack is about is giving you better memories.

By that, I don't mean giving you the tools to help you remember better. It's about making the memories you have, better.

Memories are so subjective. Two people can remember the same event completely differently. If we all remembered an event in exactly the same way, there would certainly be far fewer disagreements. We truly believe how we remember an event is how it happened.

The longer ago it was, the more chance there is for your unconscious to embellish it. Here's a perfect example: I remember when I was four, seeing a blue tin of salt in our kitchen at home. On the front of the tin was an illustration of a boy throwing salt on a bird. I asked my mother about it and she said if you threw salt on a bird, it would help you catch it.

❝ It's about making the memories you have, better. ❞ My memory is of me sitting underneath the hedge in our garden, with a handful of salt, waiting patiently for a bird to come along so that I could throw the salt over it. In my memory, my mother is watching me from the kitchen window while she does the dishes. I spoke to her about the incident, and it's true she was watching me from the window, but she wasn't doing the dishes. She couldn't have, the sink was on the other side of the kitchen.

But it was so much part of my memory. Then I thought about it some more and I realized in my memory of it, I see a view of my mum looking out of the window from inside the kitchen, which also wouldn't have been possible for me to see as I was in the garden. The more I thought about it, the more I realized I had added this image to my memory; it was as if my memory was a film, and I had edited a shot into that film.

Of course, whether my mother was washing dishes or not doesn't really have any bearing on the story, but not remembering something entirely accurately can be a very harmful thing.

In America over three hundred people have been proved to have served time for crimes they didn't commit and three-quarters of them were the result of faulty memories of witnesses.

The psychologist Elizabeth Loftus, from the University of California at Irvine, embarked upon what has turned into a decades-long examination of the ways in which misleading information can insinuate itself into one's memory.

In her most famous study, she gave two dozen subjects a journal filled with details of three events from their childhoods. To make memories as accurate and compelling as possible, Loftus enlisted family members to assemble the information. She then added a fourth, completely fictitious experience that described how, at the age of five, each child had been lost in a mall and was finally rescued by an elderly stranger. Loftus seeded the false memories with plausible information, such as the name of the mall each subject would have visited. When she interviewed the subjects later, a quarter of them recalled having been lost in the mall, and some did so in remarkable detail.

"I was crying and I remember that day … I thought I'd never see my family again", one participant said.

"Memory", says Loftus, "works a little bit like a Wikipedia page. You can go in there and change it, but so can other people."

❝ The fact our memories can and do change can be a good thing. ❞

But the fact our memories can and do change can be a good thing. And that's what this hack is about, making bad memories not so bad and good ones better.

The trouble is we have a natural bias to look for the negative in a situation. This stems back to our built-in survival instinct. It makes sense really. Once you've touched a boiling hot kettle, you don't want to do it again.

Imagine you've just written a post online and you get 20 comments. Even if 19 are really positive and only one is negative, our natural tendency is to focus on the negative one. It's why so many actors don't read reviews, because even if most of the reviews are great, it's that one negative comment that they'll keep going over in their head.

In the same way, negative memories will eat away at us. Of course, you can't get rid of memories, but how you think about them can go some way from turning a negative memory into, at the very least, a neutral memory.

Memories aren't set in stone: every time we call up a memory it changes slightly. When you remember something, your brain is "rewiring" the connections between the neurons. Literally changing the structure of your brain.

When you recall a memory you are recreating, changing, and re-memorizing. The memory is subject to change every time you remember it.

The event you remember is never going to get totally rewritten. If, for instance, you have a memory of standing in front of the whole school and forgetting what you were going to say, the event won't change; but the emotions attached to that memory can.

Daniela Schiller, who directs the laboratory for affective neuroscience at the Mount Sinai School of Medicine in New York, was working on an experiment to help people lose their fear without the use of drugs.

Up until that point, memory reconsolidation had been blocked only by either drugs or electric shocks. Dr Schiller wondered if it would be possible to reactivate a traumatic memory in humans and then block the fears associated with it.

66 When you recall a memory you are recreating, changing, and re-memorizing. The memory is subject to change every time you remember it. 99

She trained sixty-five people to have a fear of blue squares, by giving them a mild electric shock every time they were shown one.

The next day, just the sight of the square alone was enough to revive their fearful reactions. Schiller then divided the subjects into three groups. By presenting the squares many more times, with no shock, she attempted to teach them to overcome their fear. It's called extinction training. The results were dramatic: people who saw the squares within ten minutes of having their memories revived forgot their fear completely. However, the others who were not shown the squares again until hours later, remained frightened.

Strong negative memories can create strong fears and affect your attitudes and behaviour. For instance, the example of forgetting what you were going to say in front of everyone at school could create strong fears of public speaking later on in your life.

By actively thinking about the memory and trying to associate a different emotion with it, you'll reduce the negative emotion associated with it and so reduce the fear it creates.

In the example of the school speech, you could try to associate it with positive memories of the occasion, like how you laughed about the whole thing later with your friends. Try to think of a positive experience you've had of speaking in front of a group of people and associate that happier emotional memory with the school speech.

Often when we share our fears it can lessen the power they have over us. Sharing them is often easier with someone who has been through similar experiences. This shows why recovery groups like Alcoholics Anonymous are so successful.

Sometimes it only takes a small extra connection to the past to help the memories flow. For example, bilingual Russian immigrants in America could recall more autobiographical details of their early life when they were asked questions about it in Russian rather than in English.

Every memory we retain depends upon a chain of chemical interactions that connect millions of neurons to one another. Those neurons never touch; instead, they communicate through tiny gaps, or synapses, that surround each of them.

When we learn something, chemicals in the brain strengthen the synapses that connect the neurons. Long-term memories, built from new proteins, change those synaptic networks constantly. So inevitably, some grow weaker and others, as they absorb new information, grow more powerful.

It's not the 100 billion neurons in your head that are changing all the time; it's the connections between them – the neural pathways. Imagine these as real pathways across a field.

If it's a negative neural pathway every time you walk it, it's like you are wearing away the grass and creating a path that it is harder and harder to get away from. Making an effort to create positive imagery helps you step off the path and create a new positive neural pathway.

Accentuate the Positive

Now let's look at the other side of the coin, positive memories. In Britain we're not very good at accepting praise and we certainly don't feel we should wallow in it. That would be egotistical and narcissistic. But that is exactly what you should do.

The reason for spending time focusing on praise is that we need time for it to embed in our long-term memories. Then, when something happens to knock our confidence, we have positive memories about our ability to give us a boost again.

Until memories are fixed, they are fragile and easily destroyed. I know I'm terrible about remembering the names of people I've just met. I get distracted and then the name's gone.

It actually takes a few hours for new experiences to complete the biochemical and electrical process that transform them from short-term to long-term memories.

This doesn't mean you have to think about something for a couple of hours to turn it into a memory, but just focus on it for a little while so you feel confident it's joining the line for processing.

Stay with that feeling of pride in a job well done and give yourself a metaphorical pat on the back.

You can't always control what others think of you, but you do have some control over what you think of yourself.

❝ You can't always control what others think of you, but you do have some control over what you think of yourself. ❞

3 Be Kinder, Be Happier

"You can accomplish by kindness what you cannot by force."
Publilius Syrus

Once we have the basic necessities of food and shelter and being healthy, the next thing we want is to be happy.

Whether it's spending more time with family and friends, becoming rich, having a holiday, going shopping, losing weight, going for a walk in the countryside: we do all these things because we want to be happy. Of course, different people will have different opinions about which of these things will really make you happy; but we do these things because we want to be happy.

But there is an instant way to be happier, one that will also benefit others. And that is to be kind.

In a study conducted by Dr Sonja Lyubomirsky, psychology professor at University of California, Riverside, students were assigned to do five random acts of kindness per week for a period of six weeks. At the end of the study, the students' levels of happiness had increased by 41.66%.

Every thought we have and every action we take creates new connections in the brain. While, for instance, going shopping might make you feel happy for a while, it also creates the desire to do more shopping. Being kind creates a happiness that has a more long-lasting effect (and it's cheaper).

> ❝ **Every thought we have and every action we take creates new connections in the brain.** ❞

By being kind you are creating a more positive outlook, which is far more likely to make you happier.

Dr Lyubomirsky found that when describing their previous life experiences, self-nominated happy people retrospectively evaluated their experiences as more pleasant at both the time of occurrence and when recalling them. Unhappy people, however, evaluated their past life events relatively unfavourably at both time points. But what was interesting was that objective judges did not rate the events described by happy people as inherently more positive than those described by unhappy people. This suggests that happy and unhappy people experience similar events but interpret them differently.

> ❝ **Happy and unhappy people experience similar events but interpret them differently.** ❞

But being kind won't just make you happier; it can make you healthier as well. Acts of kindness are often accompanied by emotional warmth, which produces the hormone, oxytocin. Oxytocin causes the release of a chemical called nitric oxide in blood vessels, which expands the blood vessels. This in turn lowers blood pressure and therefore protects the heart. Oxytocin also reduces levels of free radicals and inflammation in the cardiovascular system. Another way it helps prevent heart disease.

In some cases it can also be good for the kidneys as well. A report in the *New England Journal of Medicine* noted that a 28-year-old man donated his kidney to a stranger in need, inspiring ten kidney donations from other donors across the US. The phrase "pay it forward" has perhaps become a bit of a cliché, but kindness really can create a ripple effect. Just think about a time when someone you didn't know did something kind and try to remember how that made you feel.

Kindness really can have a powerful effect on melting away negative emotions. A great example of this is a story regarding Nelson Mandela. After 27 years in prison, he could still show kindness to one of his oppressors who was violently opposed to everything he was trying do. At one point just before the birth of a free South Africa, Nelson Mandela entered into secret negotiations with an Afrikaner general who had been in charge of death squads. He was a man critical to the peace process because he led a large, well-armed Afrikaner resistance group. They met in Mandela's house; the general was anticipating tense negotiations across a conference table. Instead, Mandela led him to the warm, homey living room, sat beside him on a comfy couch, and spoke to him in Afrikaans. And after that, any resistance just melted away.

> ❝ **Kindness really can have a powerful effect on melting away negative emotions.** ❞

4 Reward Upfront

"Loss is nothing else but change, and change is nature's delight."

Marcus Aurelius

It's been found that people value something more once they own it.

If you give someone a bonus upfront and tell them that they'll lose it if they don't reach a specific target, they're far more likely to reach that target.

A study showed that students gained as much as a 10-percentile increase in their scores compared to students with similar backgrounds if their teacher received a bonus at the beginning of the year. The condition was that the teachers would lose the bonus if their students didn't reach a set target.

But there was found to be no gain for students when teachers were offered the bonus at the end of the school year.

It's been called "the endowment effect", but I think a better name for it is "the bird in the hand syndrome".

I remember when I was in advertising and went on a factory visit whilst working on the Mars brand. I learnt two important lessons. Firstly that too much chocolate in the hand, namely mine, made me sick and put me off chocolate for weeks. Secondly, all the Mars employees got a bonus if they clocked in before 8.30 a.m.

But rather than seeing it as a bonus for getting in early, they perceived it as their pay getting docked if they got in after 8.30 a.m.

There have been many experiments that prove this "bird in the hand syndrome". One found that students were surprisingly reluctant to trade a coffee mug they had been given for a bar of chocolate. This happened even though they did not prefer coffee mugs to chocolate when given a straight choice between the two.

It can't just be explained away as emotional attachment either. It seems it's hardwired into us. It even affects those who buy and sell for a living.

According to Pete Lunn, an economist at the Economic and Social Research Institute in Dublin, professional market traders are often reluctant to sell investments they already hold, even though they could trade them for assets they would prefer to invest in, if starting from scratch.

This "bird in the hand syndrome" can be looked at in another way: as loss aversion.

It's been found that we have a tendency to take risks when the outcome is presented as a loss, but avoid the same risks when an outcome is presented as a gain. This happens even when the objective outcome is the same.

Understanding this can have a big effect on how you communicate.

Here are some examples:

- It's much more powerful to say "Save 25%" as opposed to "Pay only 75%".
- "Stop eating foods that make you fat" will likely do better than a product that helps you "start eating foods that make you lose weight".
- Messages about how to avoid loss or pain will likely be more eye-catching and motivating than how to find pleasure of satisfaction.

Our natural tendency is always to go for the safe bet.

Something that's good to remember, not only when you're negotiating or communicating with others, but also when others are negotiating or communicating with you.

❝ Our natural tendency is always to go for the safe bet. ❞

5 Make a Better Impression

"You never get a second chance to make a first impression."
Will Rogers

In a study of 130 diner restaurants it was discovered that simply using high-quality cutlery, normally reserved for banquets, resulted in customers willing to pay 15% more for their food compared to people eating the same meal with lower quality utensils.

The research, carried out by a team from Oxford University, also showed that people eating with heavier cutlery thought food was more artistically plated and tasted better.

"It is likely that the positive or negative values that we attribute to the cutlery gets implicitly 'transferred' to our judgments of the food – a phenomenon that is often called 'sensation transference'," said Charles Michel who led the research.

This same "sensation transference" is exactly why having a good firm handshake isn't an old fashioned idea, but is actually something you will be unconsciously judged upon.

Of course, for women a firm handshake is not as important, but you could try knocking your coffee over.

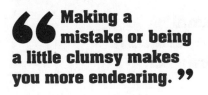 **Making a mistake or being a little clumsy makes you more endearing.** It seems making a mistake or being a little clumsy makes you more endearing. Perfection creates distance and gives off an unattractive air of invincibility.

This theory was tested by psychologist Elliot Aronson. In his test, he asked participants to listen to recordings of people answering a quiz. The recordings included the sound of the person knocking over a cup of coffee. When participants were asked to rate the quizzers on likeability they rated the people who knocked over the coffee cup as more likeable.

The "Pratfall Effect" as it's called, serves as a good reminder that it is okay to be fallible. Occasional mistakes are not only acceptable; they may turn out to be beneficial. Just so long as the mistakes are not critical.

And when it comes to your CV, make sure you print it out on really good quality paper. As your prospective employee sifts through a pile of CVs, the quality feel of the paper will really make yours stand out.

66 Occasional mistakes are not only acceptable; they may turn out to be beneficial. 99

6 Exercise More to Make Your Brain Run better

"Everywhere is within walking distance if you have the time."
Steven Wright

If you asked most people how to get a fitter, healthier brain they'd probably talk about doing brain training exercises or Sudoku.

But it's actually just as important to make your brain physically healthy, as it is about giving it mental stimulation.

Twenty minutes of vigorous activity on three or more days a week, or 30 minutes of moderate activity on five or more days a week, will reduce your chances of getting Alzheimer's by around 20%.

Even in the short-term it can have a huge effect on how your brain functions.

You know that feeling at the end of a really busy stressful day when your brain feels "fried". Well, that's because it is fried. The stress hormone cortisol is released to keep you in a state of heightened alertness. It keeps your blood sugar and blood pressure up to help you escape from danger.

In the short-term it's meant to help you deal with life-threatening situations. Getting that document finished by the end of the day is hardly life-threatening, but unfortunately you can't tell your body that.

It's called the "fight or flight" mechanism and that's why exercise is so good at countering it. You don't need to imagine you're being chased by a sabre-toothed tiger (although it might help you run a bit faster); just the act of running will help reduce the cortisol in your body. Even a brisk stroll will have a similar beneficial effect.

Most people believe it's the more cerebral activities like reading, studying and discussing that improve our minds. But as well as reducing stress, exercise has actually been proved to increase the production of grey matter in the brain.

How do you prove this when there are so many factors to be taken into account when measuring an increase in cognitive performance?

Simple really: identical twins.

It's like those old soap powder comparison ads.

"We took these two identical twins, made one sit in a chair, watch TV and eat crisps all day and make the other eat only raw vegetables and spend the whole day in the gym."

Well, that's the principle, but not something that's very practical if you want to see the effect of years of difference.

Un-Identical Identical Twins

In Finland they established something called the Finnish Twin Cohort to investigate genetic and environmental risk factors for chronic disorders. They'd created a database of over ten thousand "Finn Twins", so it was relatively easy for the University of Jyvaskyla to track down 10 sets of identical male twins – one of whom regularly exercised and one who did not.

What they found was it was not only their bodies that were different, but also their minds. Brain scans revealed that the active twins had significantly more grey matter than the sedentary twins, especially in areas of the brain involved in motor control and coordination. Amazingly, the changes in their exercise routines had mostly begun within only three years prior to the tests.

"These differences in the young men's bodies and brains had developed during their few, brief years of divergent workouts, underscoring how rapidly and robustly exercising can affect health", said Dr Urho Kujala, who oversaw the study.

So, the next time you go to the gym, remember you're not just exercising, you're brain training.

7 Let Your Body Do the Talking

"The most important thing in communication is hearing what isn't said."
Peter Drucker

Everyone's aware that your non-verbal communication has an effect on how others view you. But what's just as important is the effect it has on you.

The Fake Smile

No one likes a fake smile, but it's better than no smile at all. Frowning, grimacing, and other negative facial expressions send signals to your brain that whatever you are doing is difficult or unpleasant. This leads to your body releasing cortisol in response, which in turn raises your stress levels.

So if you make yourself smile (it doesn't have to be a full on cheesy grin), you'll feel less stressed and with the added bonus, it'll make people around you less stressed too.

Be More Determined – Cross Your Arms

If you're in someone's company and you cross your arms, they may perceive you as being defensive. But if you cross your arms when you're on your own, it can have the powerful effect of making you more determined. When you've got a difficult problem to solve, holding your arms tightly against your chest will unconsciously help you stick at it.

Stand Like Superman, Be Like Superman

It turns out all that positive psychology we often make fun of, actually does work. That doesn't mean that the next time you've got an important meeting, you should pre-empt it by standing in front of the bathroom mirror, roaring and shouting, "I'm a tiger". But the next time you've got an important meeting, interview or public speaking engagement, try power posing.

Find somewhere private and spend two minutes standing tall with your hands on your hips like Superman or Wonder Woman. You can also vary it by holding your arms out like you're addressing a crowd or holding your arms towards the sky. It seems hard to believe, but this will dramatically increase your level of confidence.

Harvard psychologist Amy Cuddy developed the idea for power posing in 2009 after hearing the former FBI agent Joe Navarro describe how police investigators would sometimes make themselves feel imposing by using a bigger chair during interrogations.

Cuddy's research has proved that if you adopt a 'power pose' for two minutes you get:

- 20% increase in testosterone (the hormone linked to dominance)
- 25% decrease in stress hormone cortisol
- Power posers were also 25% more likely to take a risk
- Reported feeling more assertive, optimistic and able to think in more abstract terms.

I think you'll agree, those are pretty good stats for just two minutes spent posing in private.

8 Be More Musical

"I live my daydreams in music. I see my life in terms of music … I get most joy in life out of music."

Einstein

If you're a musician, you're in luck. Every time you play, you're giving your brain one of the best workouts it can get. Neuroscientists have shown that musical skill requires a suite of neural processes firing in tandem: perceptual, cognitive, motor, and executive. Making a career as a musician is like being a professional bodybuilder of the mind.

Steven Pinker and others feel that our musical powers – some of them at least – are made possible by using, or recruiting, or co-opting brain systems that have already developed for other purposes. This might go with the fact that there is no single "music centre" in the human brain, but the involvement of a dozen scattered networks.

Playing music has been found to increase the volume and activity in the brain's corpus callosum – the bridge between the two hemispheres – allowing messages to get across the brain faster and through more diverse routes. This may allow musicians to solve problems more effectively and creatively, in both academic and social settings.

> **Making a career as a musician is like being a professional bodybuilder of the mind.**

So maybe Einstein's love of music was more than just a pleasant distraction from all that hard thinking he did. In actual fact, playing his violin was very much part of his working day. After a few hours thinking, he'd pick up his violin and then the ideas would start to flow. It's not surprising really as it's now been found that playing an instrument is a very good way of switching the brain from the active brain to the default mode network, "the mind-wandering brain", that's so helpful for insight.

Music can also help your brain to grow. Harvard neurologist Gottfried Schlaug found that the brains of adult professional musicians had a larger volume of grey matter than the brains of non-musicians. Schlaug and colleagues also found that after 15 months of musical training in early childhood, structural brain changes associated with motor and auditory improvements begin to appear.

In a study by Brenda Hanna-Pladdy, 70 healthy adults between the ages of 60 and 83 were divided into three groups: musicians who had studied an instrument for at least ten years, those who had played between one and nine years, and a control group who had never learned to play an instrument or how to read music. Then she had each of the subjects take a comprehensive battery of neuropsychological tests.

The group who had studied for at least ten years scored the highest in such areas as nonverbal and visuospatial memory, naming objects, and taking in and adapting new information. By contrast, those with no musical training performed least well, and those who had played between one and nine years were in the middle.

In other words, the more they had trained and played, the more benefit the participants had gained. But, intriguingly, they didn't lose all of the benefits even when they hadn't played music in decades.

And it's not too late to gain the benefits, even if you don't take up an instrument until later in life. Jennifer Burgos, an assistant professor of music education at the University of South Florida, Tampa, studied the impact of individual piano instruction on adults between the ages of 60 and 85. After six months, those who had received piano lessons showed more robust gains in memory, verbal fluency, the speed at which they processed information, planning ability, and other cognitive functions, compared with those who had not received lessons.

"Musical training seems to have a beneficial impact at whatever age you start. It contains all the components of a cognitive training program that sometimes are overlooked, and just as we work out our bodies, we should work out our minds," she says.

So if you want the keys to a fitter, stronger, more active mind, they're piano keys.

9 Don't Get Labelled

"What's in a name? that which we call a rose
by any other name would smell as sweet."
William Shakespeare

WARNING!
WARNING!
WARNING!

**YOUR BRAIN IS
BEING HACKED!**

Wouldn't it be nice if we got a warning like this every time we were
unconsciously influenced by things around us? That's the aim of this hack.
It's not about how you control your brain, but how outside influences
control it.

Sticks and Stones May Break Your Bones, but Words They Can Control You

Language and how it is used has a very powerful effect on us.

I've often thought that when visiting websites, we more readily "accept cookies" because of the language used. Cookies collect data on the sites we use and also if you are buying something, your credit card details. Until the Internet came along, the only association with the term "cookies" was biscuits – and who doesn't like biscuits?

I'm sure that the previous positive association has an effect. Imagine how differently we'd feel if every time we went to a site and the message popped up, "Do you accept shadowing?". Of course, the word "cookies" wasn't called this to be less sinister; it actually derives from UNIX objects called "magic cookies". Imagine if they used that? Who could refuse the offer of magic cookies?

These are just my thoughts, but there are very real and scary examples of language having a strong effect on people's decisions.

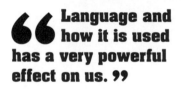 **Language and how it is used has a very powerful effect on us. 99**

In an experiment, people were shown a simulated accident and then asked about the speed the cars were going when the accident happened.

When asked what speed the cars were going when they "hit" each other, the average was 34 mph.

When asked what speed the cars were going when they "smashed" into each other, the average speed was 41 mph.

People were influenced not just by what they saw, but the language the questioner used.

They were also asked if there was broken glass at the accident. When the question was asked with the word "hit" 14% said there was, when it was asked with "smashed" 32% said it was. In fact, there was no broken glass at all. Even just the fact that the question was asked, made people believe there was broken glass.

What's in a Name?

When I was growing up there were no famous people called Neil, so when my namesake Neil Armstrong came to fame you can imagine my excitement. He wasn't just the first man on the moon he was the first "Neil" on the moon.

That's one small step for man, one giant leap for Neils.

But this attraction to any link to our own name isn't something we grow out of, it's just something we become less conscious of.

As I'm sure you know, hurricanes are named after people and in alphabetical order.

Researchers examined Red Cross donation records following seven catastrophic Atlantic Ocean hurricanes that hit the United States between 1998 and 2005.

For example, people with K names donated 4% to all disasters before Katrina devastated New Orleans in 2005. But then when Katrina hit, 10% of all the donations came from K-named people, a 150% increase.

The same were true for a range of hurricanes as this graph shows:

This is called nominative determinism, which means "name-driven outcome".

People are also unconsciously more likely to choose a road to live on that starts with the same letter as their name starts with. People are even more likely to do a job that has some connection to their name.

It sounds like a joke but two urology experts, A.J. Splatt and D. Weedon, have written a paper on the problem of painful urination in the *British Journal of Urology*.

The former Lord Chief Justice of England and Wales was Igor Judge. A man called Justice Laws, better known as the Right Honorable Justice Laws, is a Lord Justice of Appeal.

Another unconscious way a name affects our actions is where your name comes in the alphabet. This harks back to our schooldays, where people with N–Z names habitually wait behind people with A–M names, so making them more impatient. In my days it was surnames and now it's Christian names, but the principle's the same.

> **People are even more likely to do a job that has some connection to their name.**

Researchers found that N to Z'ers were quicker to respond to limited opportunities because they so often had to wait their turn.

When a limited number of free basketball tickets were offered to a group of graduate students, the further down the list they were, the quicker they were to respond. In another study, the researchers found that PhD students with later letter names were quicker to post their job-search materials online than the students with earlier letter names.

Even in business, the sound of a company's name can have a powerful effect. A study in 1979 found that 38 of the top two hundred US brand names began with the dominant sounds K or C, and as many as ninety-three of them contained the 'k' sound somewhere in their names.

Maluma or Takete

Now look at these two shapes below. One of them is called "takete" and one is called "maluma", which one do you think is which?

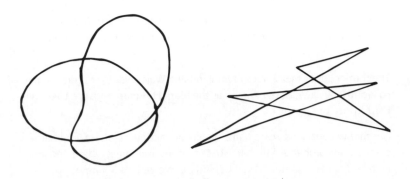

The majority of people say the one on the left is maluma and the one on the right is takete. And it's not just the way the word looks; it's the way the word sounds. Even pre-school children who can't read, match up maluma with the round, soft-edged picture and takete with the jagged, spiky-shaped picture.

This test is from a famous 1920's textbook by German psychologist Wolfgang Köhler on how we perceive the world. This example (which also crosses language barriers) shows that certain words sound soft and gentle and others sound hard and jagged.

It could be worth considering if you are naming a new company or product as to whether you want it to be a bit "maluma" (soft, gentle, friendly, approachable, creative) or a bit more "takete" (sharp, hard-nosed, straightforward, focused, competitive). These qualities tie in with why so many of the top US brand names have a hard "K" sound in their name.

It's easier to categorize relatively new companies. With older companies there are so many factors that affect your judgement of them.

Here are some examples:

Takete companies
Nike
Netflix
Starbucks
Viacom
Lexmark

Maluma companies
Google
Apple
Pepsi
Oracle
Ebay

Nominative determinism even relates to people. Now that celebrities are becoming brands, it's interesting to see when they have changed their name, who has changed from a softer "maluma" name to an edgier "takete" name and vice versa:

Maluma to Takete
Eric Marlon Bishop to Jamie Foxx
Laura Hollins to Agyness Deyn
Eilleen Regina Edwards to Shania Twain

Takete to Maluma
Lizzie Grant to Lana Del Rey
Audrey Ruston to Audrey Hepburn
Neta-Lee Hershlag to Natalie Portman

So whether it's for a company, a brand or a person, a name is never just a name.

❝ A name is never just a name. ❞

PART 2

Getting Started

How to use your time better and be more productive

10 See Things Differently

"The more I see, the less I know for sure."
John Lennon

How we think we see the world, is not always how it is. Here are just a few examples of some visual ways our brains are hacked.

An Uphill Battle

You would have thought when looking at a map, it would be pretty obvious to tell which place was nearer and which was farther away.

But just the language we use about locations can have an effect on how we view their geography. When we talk about going somewhere in a northerly direction we use "up". If you live in London you'd say I'm going "up North" or "up to Scotland". Now this may seem innocuous enough, but believe it or not, by saying "up" you unconsciously feel it's going to be uphill.

In one experiment in America, people were asked how much they thought a delivery company would charge for delivering an item between two locations. What they found, was there was a big difference depending on whether the trip was northbound or southbound. When it was a northbound trip people believed a delivery company would charge $235 more. Unconsciously, they felt the trip was "uphill" and therefore would require more effort and petrol.

A second group of people were more willing to drive to a shop located five miles south from the city centre, rather than five miles north. Again because reaching the northerly shop was thought to demand more effort than reaching the southerly shop.

We've Got Our Eyes on You

For several years the kitchen in the psychology department at Newcastle University had an honesty box asking people to pay a small fee for tea and coffee. The pile of coins in the honesty box accumulated slowly, while the tea, coffee and milk supplies shrank rapidly. Melissa Bateson and her colleagues were getting a bit fed up with this. But being a psychology department, rather than just saying something, they decided to run their own little experiment:

For a ten-week period, they displayed different pictures above the price list. Each week, they alternated between images of flowers and a pair of staring eyes.

When the image featured the eyes, people unconsciously felt they were being watched and paid an average of three times as much.

Think of a Colour

It may be nothing more than an association with big skies and the open sea, but seeing the colour blue or working in a blue environment has been proved to make you more creative.

Juliet Zhu at the University of British Columbia in Vancouver compared the effects of red and blue on people's behaviour. While red tended to sharpen the memories of her undergraduate volunteers, blue helped to unlock their imaginations.

For example, when they were given toy parts in either blue or red, the toys that the volunteers constructed in blue were rated as much more creative. Twelve judges saw greyscale versions of the designs and rated them in terms of practicality and appropriateness (reflecting attention to detail) and originality (representing a creative streak).

> **Seeing the colour blue or working in a blue environment has been proved to make you more creative.**

The judges' verdicts were largely in agreement – toys built from red parts were deemed more practical and appropriate than those built from blue parts, but less novel or original.

I actually chose blue illustrations for this book in the hope it would help stimulate your imagination and make you more engaged in the ideas in it. Not exactly brainwashing – more of a brain-rinse.

In the tests, however, red boosted performance on detail-oriented tasks such as memory retrieval and proofreading by as much as 31% compared to blue.

Of course, it also depends on environment. In Glasgow, they wanted to make the city look more beautiful at night by installing blue lighting in prominent locations. Although it was never the intention, this blue light had a powerful effect of reducing crime in these areas. They realized that the blue light, which is the same as the blue light from police cars, unconsciously made people feel that in those areas the police were watching them.

In 1979, Professor Alexander Schauss described a simple experiment where he got healthy young men to stare at one of two pieces of cardboard. For half the men the cardboard was the colour of deep blue, while for the other half, it was bright pink. After a full minute had passed, the men were asked to squeeze a measurement device known as a dynamometer. They then spent a minute staring at the other colour. Without fail, one after another, all thirty-eight men squeezed the device more weakly after staring at the pink cardboard, proving that the colour pink has a strong tranquilizing effect.

It just goes to show that whatever we think, how we truly see the world is never black and white.

> **" It just goes to show that whatever we think, how we truly see the world is never black and white. "**

11   Watch Cat Videos

"Always laugh when you can. It is cheap medicine."
Lord Byron

In a recent study by the Draugiem Group it was found that the 10% of employees with the highest productivity, surprisingly didn't put in longer hours than anyone else. In fact, they didn't even work full eight-hour days. What they did do was take regular breaks. Specifically, they took 17-minute breaks for every 52 minutes of work.

And to be really productive, it's just as important to concentrate on what you do in your breaks as what you do while you're working.

Laughing All the Way to the Bank

Once you've stretched your legs and got yourself a coffee, the last thing you should do is sit down at your desk and check up on what's happening in the news. What you should be doing is sitting down at your desk and watching videos of epic fails, grumpy cats and sneezing pandas; whatever makes you laugh, in fact.

A study published in the journal *Psychological Science* found that subjects who watched brief video clips that made them feel sad were less able to solve problems creatively than people who watched an upbeat video.

Ruby Nadler, one of the researchers from the University of Western Ontario said, "A positive mood increases cognitive flexibility, while a negative mood narrows our mental horizons. If you have a project where you want to think innovatively, or you have a problem to carefully consider, being in a positive mood can help you to do that."

One of the other great benefits of watching things that make you laugh is that they're fantastic stress busters.

> **One of the other great benefits of watching things that make you laugh is that they're fantastic stress busters.**

Seeing a Joke Coming

Dr Lee Berk and his team at Loma Linda University in California ran tests on the effects of watching funny videos in relation to reducing stress.

The tests showed that thirty minutes after watching funny videos, cortisol was down 67%, adrenaline was down 35%, and DOPAC was down 69%.

But what really shocked the team was that cortisol, adrenaline and DOPAC decreased by 39%, 70%, and 38% respectively before anything funny was seen. "It would seem that merely having a merry heart in anticipation of the happy experience, lowers stress levels," said Dr Berk.

Now this cat may look grumpy, but I'm sure if he knew the huge positive impact he was having on the country's workforce, he'd realize the humiliation of having to wear a bunny outfit was a small price to pay.

**'I'm not grumpy, I'm livid.
I specifically ordered the tiger onesie.'**

12 Don't Be Biased

> "The human understanding when it has once adopted an opinion (either as being the received opinion or as being agreeable to itself) draws all things else to support and agree with it."
>
> *Francis Bacon*

How biased are you?

You might think you're not that biased, but you are, we all are.

Cognitive bias is the way our mind skews our thinking or decisions. If you look up cognitive bias on Wikipedia, there is a list of over a hundred. There is even one called "the IKEA effect: The tendency for people to place a disproportionately high value on objects that they partially assembled themselves, such as furniture from IKEA, regardless of the quality of the end result".

Some social psychologists believe our cognitive biases help us process information more efficiently, especially in dangerous situations. The trouble is these biases still happen when we're not in danger and can often lead to serious errors in judgement (like buying furniture that you have to assemble yourself!).

Often, the more experienced you are in a field, the more biased you become. A classic example of this created the central premise for the book and the film *Moneyball*. It showed the collected wisdom of baseball insiders (including players, managers, coaches, scouts, and the front office) over the past century is subjective and often flawed. Statistics such as stolen bases, runs batted in and batting average typically used to gauge players, are relics of a 19th-century view of the game and the statistics available at that time.

The Oakland A's used a more analytical gauge of player performance to field a team that successfully competed with the big teams like New York Yankees who had a payroll of three times as much.

❝ The more experienced you are in a field, the more biased you become. ❞

You Be the Judge

Bias can be caused by so many different factors. In the following example, it is not by something lacking in the brain, but by something lacking in the stomach.

A study in 2011[1] showed that judges in Israel were far more lenient straight after meal breaks, but became harsher as the time elapsed since their last break increased (denying parole requests with higher frequency). Parole applicants were clearly treated differently depending on when their cases came up. This is pretty shocking, but at least the bias can easily be counteracted by simply creating more breaks.

Now I want to test your bias.

Think about how you felt when you read that last paragraph. Did the fact that they were "Israeli" judges have any negative or positive effect on you? The thing is, people have quite polarized views about Israel and this can add bias.

In actual fact, it's irrelevant that the judges were Israeli, it's just that the study happened to take place there. The findings would have no doubt been the same in any country where there weren't enough breaks in court sessions.

Still on the subject of food, but on a more personal level, there is another bias called "the current moment bias". This is based on the fact that we have a really hard time imagining ourselves in the future and alter our behaviour and expectations accordingly.

A 1998 study[2] showed that, when making food choices for the coming week, 74% of participants chose fruit. But when the food choice was for the current day, 70% chose chocolate.

Now you might think you would be less biased than that. But then you would, wouldn't you?

In fact we all (well, nearly all) would. Only one in every 166 people believes they are more biased than the average person. It's what's called the bias blind spot. It's the tendency to see ourselves as less biased than other people.

Biased About Our Own Bias

Take doctors for example. When they receive gifts from pharmaceutical companies, they may claim that the gifts don't affect their decisions about what medicine to prescribe because they have no memory of the gifts biasing their prescriptions. However, if you ask them whether a gift might unconsciously bias the decisions of other doctors, most will agree that other doctors are unconsciously biased by the gifts, while continuing to believe that their own decisions are not.[3]

"People seem to have no idea how biased they are. Whether a good decision-maker or a bad one, everyone thinks that they are less biased than their peers," said Carey Morewedge, associate professor of marketing at Boston University. "This susceptibility to the bias blind spot appears to be pervasive, and is unrelated to people's intelligence, self-esteem, and actual ability to make unbiased judgments and decisions."

The trouble with this bias blind spot is we can try to push ideas through, even if they aren't very good, purely because we thought of them. That's why it's always good to get the opinion of someone you trust on your ideas or projects.

> ❝ It's always good to get the opinion of someone you trust on your ideas or projects. ❞

The strength of the blind spot bias will show through because what you're really asking them is to confirm what you believe, that it's a great idea. If they're lukewarm about the idea, the first thing you question is their judgement and not your idea.

Another way to counteract your personal bias yourself, is to give it time. Put your idea to one side and carry on thinking. When you come back to it later, you'll find you will be able to judge it in a more unbiased way.

Julia Galef who runs courses on the science of decision-making says, "It's so easy to see the silliness in other people's thinking, but so hard to see the problems in our own."

She came up with an idea to shock herself out of making biased decisions. A "Surprise Journal". She keeps this journal with her at all times, writing down when something surprises her and why. Whether it is a negative or positive response to her presentations or ideas, if it surprises her, she makes a note of it.

By being interested in the surprise and not taking the negative or positive reaction personally, she can counteract the bias blind spot.

She says the act of carrying a Surprise Journal around causes her to notice when things strike her as odd or unusual. Sometimes, it surprises her when audience members seem enthusiastic about one of her talks. But rather than just being flattered by the positive feedback, Galef uses it as an opportunity to assess her own understanding of what makes a topic useful or interesting.

I think this is a great idea, although I think my idea of getting feedback from someone you trust is even better. But then I might be biased.

13 Practice With Purpose

"Don't practice until you get it right. Practice until you can't get it wrong."

Unknown

I'm sure you're aware of the 10,000-hour theory made famous by Malcolm Gladwell, in which he argues that to become truly great at anything you need to spend at least 10,000 hours doing it.

But it doesn't mean that just because you spend 10,000 hours doing something, you're going to become great at it. Obviously you do need to spend time working at it, but it's how you spend that time that really counts.

It shouldn't be practice makes perfect, it should be the right practice makes perfect.

If you do the same thing over and over again, once you get past a certain level you're not going to be learning anything new.

Do you want to learn to ride a bike, or do you want to learn how to do a wheelie?

In *The Karate Kid* (I'm really showing the depth of my cultural knowledge here), a bullied boy (Daniel) is rescued from a beating by Mr Miyagi, an elderly gardener. He asks Mr Miyagi to teach him karate. But what does Mr Miyagi have him do first? See how high he can kick? No, wax cars.

Daniel thinks he's wasting his time, but later realizes that what he thought were pointless skills have taught him about movement of his arms and balance. Both of which are vital to him later on.

> **It shouldn't be practice makes perfect, it should be the right practice makes perfect.**

"Deliberate practice" is about pushing yourself beyond your comfort zone, but it's also about learning from it.

Two researchers, Timothy J. Cleary and Barry J. Zimmerman from the City University of New York, did a study of basketball players to see if they

could discern a difference between the practice habits of the best free throw shooters (70% or higher) and the worst free throw shooters (55% or lower).

The two main differences were these:

1. The best free throw shooters had specific goals about what they wanted to accomplish or focus on before they made a practice free throw attempt. As in, "I'm going to make 10 out of 10 shots" or "I'm going to keep my elbows in".

The worst free throw shooters had the simple goal of just "making the shot".

2. Invariably, the players would miss shots now and again, but when the best free throw shooters missed, they tended to attribute their miss to specific technical problems, like "I didn't bend my knees". This lends itself to a more specific goal for the next practice attempt, and a more thoughtful reflection process upon the hit or miss of the subsequent free throw.

In contrast, the worst performers were more likely to attribute failure to non-specific factors, like "My rhythm was off" or "I wasn't focused" which doesn't do much to inform the next practice attempt.

You want to create new neural pathways, so it's also about training and learning in different ways.

Music is another area, where how you practice is vital. The difference between a good violinist and a great one is the quality and concentration of the time they spend practising, not the length. In fact, it was found that the elite musicians actually practised less, slept more and were less stressed.

Just doing the same thing over and over again, isn't going to create fresh neural pathways in the brain. It's the intensity and focus that hacks the brain into learning and remembering new things.

Violinist Nathan Milstein noticed other students around him practising all day, and asked his mentor how many hours a day he should be practising. His mentor replied, "It doesn't really matter how long. If you practise with your fingers, no amount is enough. If you practise with your head, two hours is plenty."

When most musicians sit down to practise, they play the parts of pieces that they're good at. But expert musicians tend to focus on the parts that are hard, the parts they haven't yet mastered.

Elite musicians don't:

- Go though their music without concentration.
- Repeat skills they have already mastered.
- Allow themselves to repeat or "get by" with mistakes, so that these become engrained in their muscle memory.

Their aim is to reach a level just beyond the currently attainable level of performance by engaging in:

- Being very focused.
- Analysing what they've done after getting feedback and how they can do it better.
- Repeating areas of weakness and making constant refinements.

Whether it's in the arts, sports or business, "deliberate practice" will have the strongest effect on your brain and therefore have the strongest effect on your future ability.

66 **Deliberate practice will have the strongest effect on your brain.** **99**

14 Stop Moaning

"What you're supposed to do when you don't like a thing is change it. If you can't change it, change the way you think about it. Don't complain."

Maya Angelou

Everyone likes a bit of a moan, especially in Britain. We don't like to complain, but we like to moan.

We moan as a way of letting off steam when we've had a confrontation at work, someone's been rude or we've got angry about bad service or being treated unfairly.

But moaning can also unite us. It's an ice-breaker, a way of creating a bond with someone you don't know. Say you get in a taxi; you can immediately start a conversation by moaning about the weather or the traffic.

"It's one way to create rapport", said Joanna Wolfe, a professor of English at Carnegie Mellon University whose research focuses on communication styles. Complaining about a late bus with other passengers, for instance, "creates kind of a solidarity", she said.

The trouble is if we moan too much it can be really bad for us.

The thing is, we see it more as a way of letting off steam than as negative energy. If someone told you about a person who was extremely negative, you probably wouldn't be that keen to meet that person. You'd think their negativity would just bring you down. But when we "have a bit of a moan", we don't really see it as being particularly negative, more of just a need to chat about something that's been bugging you.

But unfortunately even just the smallest of moans is still a negative thought. It may feel like you're just getting something off your chest, but you're sending it straight to your brain. Because when we moan it creates the stress hormone, cortisol. And cortisol has a bad effect on the hippocampus, which is highly sensitive to negative stimuli.

66 Even just the smallest of moans is still a negative thought. 99

The hippocampus is the area in our brain that deals with the formation of long-term memories and spatial navigation and also one of the few regions able to produce new neurons. Severe damage to the hippocampus leads to memory loss as in Alzheimer's and can also lead to the inability to form new memories.

Robert Sapolsky, a professor of neurology and neuroendocrinology at Stanford University's School of Medicine, has done extensive research on the effect of stress on the hippocampus and has found that moaning for more than 30 minutes leads to elevated cortisol levels that hamper synaptic connections and speed up cell death. Over time, repeated bouts of negativity will cause the hippocampus to shrink, resulting in "declines in cognitive function, including the ability to retain information and adapt to new situations".

If that's not bad enough, you're not just affected by moaning, you're also affected by listening to someone moan.

Of course stopping moaning completely would be incredibly hard. Thierry Blancpain and Pieter Pelgrims started the Complaint Restraint project (complaintrestraint .com), a project to help people create a more positive life by eliminating negative statements. They've blocked out February (because it's the shortest) as a month to try not to moan. But they freely admit they fail their mission miserably every year. Things we do habitually are really hard to break free from, but that doesn't mean we shouldn't try.

We all need to have a bit of a moan at times. In fact, research has shown that if we do keep things bottled up, it can reduce our life by up to two years. The aim is just to reduce the amount we moan.

Don't Moan. Complain

One thing you actually can do is to complain instead of moan. Complaining is a positive action and is much more likely to get a gripe out of your system.

Say, for example, your train was delayed for the third day in a row. By calling up the train company or writing them an email, you've acted, and just by doing this, your annoyance at it will subside. If you moan about it, it doesn't make your annoyance subside, if anything it adds fuel to the fire.

You can actually feel the difference between complaining and moaning. Take the train scenario for instance. First try to imagine you're talking on the phone to someone from customer service at the train company and imagine the conversation you would have. Okay, now try imagining you haven't complained, but you're moaning to a friend at work about the terrible train service.

I don't know about you, but when I did this I really noticed the difference. When I imagined myself complaining to customer service, I don't know if I felt angry exactly, more of a righteous indignation and a forceful energy. When I then imagined myself just moaning to a friend, I actually felt my shoulders drop and definitely felt more negative. I had to fight to stop myself shaking my head from side to side. Even if you didn't feel exactly like that, it's interesting to feel the difference between the two.

> **❝ One thing you actually can do is to complain instead of moan. ❞**

But the trouble is we usually moan rather than complain. Dr Guy Winch, a psychologist and author of *The Squeaky Wheel* says that research has found that 95% of consumers who have a problem with a product don't complain to the company, but they will moan about it to between 8 to 16 people.

"We tell ourselves that we need to get it off our chest, but each time we do, we get upset all over again and end up 10 to 12 times more aggravated," says Dr Winch.

How To Complain

So to get the problem off your chest it's best to complain about it, but it's important to know the right way to complain. If you don't, when you're unsuccessful, it'll just give you something extra to moan about – and that's the last thing you want.

Dr Winch says complaining the right way may not only create a solution; it can curb anxiety and improve relationships. He offers these seven tips:

A complaint should have a purpose

Before you share your woes, have a specific goal in mind.

The more you think about what you want to achieve, the more rational and level-headed you'll be.

It makes it easier for the person dealing with your complaint. If you don't know what you want, the other person may not know how to resolve the situation.

"Identifying a purpose is most important when complaining to a spouse, friend, or colleague," says Dr Winch, "because this is when you're likely to take the least amount of time preparing. Don't voice dissatisfaction until you're clear about why you're upset and what you want."

Start with a positive statement

Before you launch into the problem, set the stage for a positive outcome. Even customer service professionals will get defensive if you start out in anger.

"A complaint is an accusation," says Dr Winch. "It's natural to get defensive, but you want to deliver your complaint in a way that motivates the other person to help."

State something positive, such as the fact that you've been a loyal customer or that you share a common goal. This makes the person less defensive and more likely to listen to what you say next.

Deliver a lean complaint

"If the problem has been going on for a while, don't go into each and every detail," says Winch. Instead, talk about the most recent incident. Stick to the facts as much as possible and hold back on emotions.

4 End with another positive statement

Finish your complaint by ending on a high note. Tell the person if the problem is resolved, then it will improve your relationship. Or simply say something like, "I would really appreciate your help."

Dr Winch says wrapping your complaint between two positive statements builds a complaint sandwich that's easier to swallow: "When you add in the positives, you're more likely to get the result you want. The person will find you much more pleasant to deal with, and they'll be more motivated to use their resources to help you than if they feel abused because you were having a go at them."

5 Consider your listener

If you are complaining to a company, remember the person you're talking to probably didn't make the product or the company policies.

"A complaint is a request for help and when we ask for help, we ask nicely," says Winch. "This can be tricky because we are not motivated to be nice when we are most annoyed."

If you can't control your emotions, then at least acknowledge them. "Tell them, 'I'm sorry if I sound annoyed; it's not you,'" says Winch. "Let them know it's not personal. They will appreciate that."

6 Use social media properly

Complaining on social media can be effective because many companies monitor their accounts.

"If you complain on Twitter or Facebook, you're likely to get a helpful response if you provide enough information for them to contact you," says Dr Winch. "If your flight was cancelled for example, you might get immediate results by posting your problem on Twitter rather than standing in line with everyone else for 45 minutes."

7 Let it go

Whatever the outcome, be prepared to let it go instead of dwelling on it. Taking the time to complain properly can help.

If you have done all you can, it will be easier for you to mentally close the case.

"Get" Your "But" Into Gear

You can't complain about everything, but you can stop yourself moaning about it. Here are two tips that might help. Imagine you've got a boring document to write:

1. "But-Positive" – If you find yourself moaning "I've got this really boring document to write" add but on the end with a positive thought: "I've got this really boring document to write, but at least once I've done it, I won't have it hanging over me.

2. Change "have to" to "get to" – You change a moaning voice, that implies whatever it is you have no choice in the matter, to a more empowered voice. Change "I can't come out to lunch I have to write this boring document" to "I can't come out to lunch, because if I get to write this boring document now, then it's out of the way."

15 Don't Get Stressed

> "We must have a pie. Stress cannot exist
> in the presence of a pie."
> *David Mamet, Boston Marriage*

When you hear the phrase "performance-enhancing drugs", you probably start thinking about the darker side of top level sport. But the fact is we're all affected by them.

Cortisol (as I've previously mentioned) is most commonly linked to stress, but it is in actual fact a performance-enhancing steroid hormone. (Yes, you're on steroids as well.) Its main purpose is to increase blood pressure and blood sugar, to give us focus and energy. The trouble begins though, when we start worrying.

According to most studies, public speaking is people's number one fear. Number two is death! As Jerry Seinfeld said, "This means to the average person, if you go to a funeral, you're better off in the casket than doing the eulogy."

Whether it's having to give a speech, organizing a big event or meeting a certain deadline, you need a boost.

You want focused performance energy, but you don't want the worry – the performance anxiety. The trouble is, your adrenal gland can't tell the difference between you needing the energy at work, to you worrying about it at night. The cortisol tap gets turned on and left on and that's when you get all those negative effects that are associated with stress.

One of the problems is that we call it stress. The word "stress" has so many negative connotations, that when we tell ourselves we're stressed, it's just going to make it worse.

Take the term "performance energy" – it sounds like a good thing doesn't it? Well, stress is just performance energy that's outstayed its welcome.

So the first thing is to forget about stress and think instead how to control your performance energy and make it work for you.

Turn Performance Anxiety into Performance Energy

To start with, we often spend too much time thinking and not enough time planning and doing.

The danger is that the time we spend thinking leads to self-critical thoughts, which leads to stress, which leads to a big hit of cortisol and the next thing you know you're bent over double, breathing into a paper bag.

If you've got a project to finish, don't worry about whether you're going to finish it or not, just get to work on it. If you've got a speech or presentation to make, don't imagine how it's going to go, just write down what you're going to say and practise it.

Keep focusing on what you're going to say and not the event itself. If you are starting to get nervous, practising what you're going to say gives your performance energy somewhere to go.

> **❝ We often spend too much time thinking and not enough time planning and doing. ❞**

If you ever see a stand-up comedian perform on different nights, you'll be amazed at how similar the performances are. All those moments that felt improvised and spontaneous are often written. They've sweated over every single word. Now I'm not saying you have to go to those lengths but being well prepared will make you feel more confident and help you relax.

Of course there will inevitably be times when self-critical thoughts will creep into your head and you'll start feeling anxious. If this happens it's good to have a few tricks up your sleeve.

First, try reading. In tests at Sussex University, cognitive neuropsychologist Dr David Lewis found that it reduced stress by 68%. Subjects only needed to read silently for six minutes to slow down the heart rate and ease tension in the muscles. In fact, he said, it took their stress levels to lower than before they started the test.

Listening to music reduced the levels by 61%, having a cup of tea or coffee lowered them by 54% and taking a walk by 42%.

You could also try eating dark chocolate, which is a proven stress buster. So "death by chocolate" cake does

kill. It murders stress. Maybe that's why stressed backwards spells desserts.

But what's most important is to be well prepared. If you really want to challenge yourself you can create the symptoms of performance energy. Run up and down the stairs a couple of times and then once you've got your breath back, try running through what's causing you to be stressed. The increase in blood pressure, will at least give you a feel of what it will be like on the big day.

❝❝ What's most important is to be well prepared. ❞❞

It's all about giving you confidence and helping you feel relaxed in the lead up to whatever upcoming event you're getting stressed about.

Keep practising and not thinking. Then when the time comes, you'll have the focus of performance energy and not the stress of performance anxiety.

STRESSED

BACKWARDS SPELLS

DESSERTS

16 Make Fewer Decisions

> "An expert is someone who has succeeded in making decisions and judgements simpler through knowing what to pay attention to and what to ignore."
> *Edward De Bono*

Every time we have to make a decision, it is resolved in the courtroom of our brains. Sights, sounds and other sensory evidence are registered by the sensory circuits. Then various neurons act like the "jury", collating and weighing up each piece of evidence. Finally a decision is made.

And as we normally have to make thousands of decisions each day, it's not surprising that we often feel mentally drained by the end of it. This is just one of the reasons why it's so important to get a good night's sleep, as it has the effect of completely recharging our brains.

The fact that every choice you make is going to use up a little bit of your energy is why a lot of successful people reduce the amount of daily decisions they have to make.

In a recent online Q&A session with Facebook CEO Mark Zuckerberg,[1] there was one question quite a few people had on their minds: why does he always wear a dark grey T-shirt?

It's not a question that's on his mind of course, because he's decided not to think about what he wears every day. Zuckerberg said "I'm not doing my job if I spend any of my energy on things that are silly or frivolous about my life."

> **A lot of successful people reduce the amount of daily decisions they have to make.**

He's not the only one. Barack Obama is almost always seen in grey or blue suits. He says, "I don't want to make decisions about what I'm eating or wearing. Because I have too many other decisions to make."

Steve Jobs was famous for his black crew neck jumpers, jeans and trainers. He once even tried to get Apple staff to wear a type of uniform, but the idea didn't go down very well. iClothes anyone?

And it's not just men who have taken up this move to sartorial simplification. For the past three years, New York art director Matilda Kahl[2] has been wearing the same outfit to work every single day.

She said she was tired of running late in the morning, re-evaluating her outfits, and stressing about whether her clothes were appropriate for different events or meetings at her advertising agency. For someone in the creative field who has to make a lot of decisions throughout the day, she longed for one less choice to make.

After a couple of days of searching she found the perfect work uniform and bought 15 versions of the same white silk top as well as six pairs of black trousers.

Of course, the problem is not just about the amount of decisions we have to make, but also the number of options we have to choose from in each decision. There's no denying having a choice is a good thing, but there can be such a thing as too much choice.

The author of *The Paradox Of Choice,* psychologist Barry Schwartz, says that too much choice can actually lead to paralysis.

In a study that was done into voluntary retirement plans in big companies, it was found that for every ten extra mutual funds that employees were offered, the rate of participation went down by 2%. Too much choice can just be too overwhelming, so we end up just not making a choice at all.

The other negative linked with more choice is that it increases your expectations. When you've had so many options to choose from, you expect the one you've chosen to be perfect. When it's not, this leads to more dissatisfaction than if you'd had less choice in the first place.

In an interview on the subject for the FT, neuroscientist Dr Tara Swart said, "There is only so much quality thinking your brain can do each day. Every time you make a decision, wrestle with a problem or think creatively, you use it up. Then you become vulnerable to decision fatigue, which is when your weary brain makes poor decisions or none at all." [3]

" Too much choice can just be too overwhelming, so we end up just not making a choice at all. "

This basically means that if you want to save your brainpower for important decisions or creative problem solving, limit what you have to think about every morning. Narrow down your choice of clothes, get up at the same time, have the same morning routine. Your brain's at its sharpest in the morning, so don't dull it by humming and hawing over which cereal to have for breakfast.

While choice reduction can be really helpful, you shouldn't be too strict with yourself. When you're not so busy and at the weekends, making choices will actually become more enjoyable.

Even after her "office uniform" experiment, Matilda Kahl says she still likes choosing what to wear on weekends and weeknights. "Nowadays, I never have to rush through the process of putting together an outfit, so the whole experience has become a lot more enjoyable. It has really made me more appreciative of the clothes I own – they feel more special now when I don't wear them every day."

Whether you decide to have a very strict routine or not, what's most important is that you're in control of choosing when you have a choice.

17 Count the Days, Minutes and Hours

"Time is what we want most, but what we use worst."
William Penn

Why is it so hard to keep New Year's resolutions?

It's not to do with our goals being unachievable, it's because we call them "New Year resolutions". If we called them "New Day resolutions" or even "New Month resolutions", we'd be far more likely to keep to them.

The reason for this is that the smaller the unit of time a task is expressed in, the closer it seems and so the more likely you are to start working on it.

For instance, if you have a project deadline of three months, it's better to express it as ninety days. Or if you have something you need to complete in three days, think of your deadline as 72 hours away.

This was discovered in a study by the University of Southern California, lead by Dr Daphna Oyserman.

"People focus most of their attention on the present, which is for sure, rather than on the future, which is possible and may need our attention later," Dr Oyserman said. "The present takes precedence."

66 If we called them "New Day resolutions" or even "New Month resolutions", we'd be far more likely to keep to them. 99

In one experiment, 162 study participants were asked to imagine themselves preparing for a future event, such as a wedding or work presentation, and then told to consider the event in either days, months or years away. Those who thought about the time until the event in terms of days imagined that it would occur an average of 30 days earlier than those who thought in terms of months or years.

In another experiment, 1,100 participants were asked when they would start saving money for retirement. Some participants were told they would retire 30 or 40 years from now, others that their work life would end in 10,950 or 14,600 days.

Incredibly, they found that people were likely to start saving four times sooner when the time until the event was expressed in days rather than years.

"The technique is effective even when the goal is very far away, because people tend to focus more on the unit of time," says Oyserman.

It's all about a task being more urgent and needing our attention. If you had a resolution that in the next year you'll get fit, it's far more likely that you'll be successful if you say that you're going to get fit in the next 365 days. If it's expressed in days, you might even add some action like go for a run to your daily to-do list, which you're unlikely to do if the goal's expressed as a year.

"When you use days rather than years, it makes you feel like the future is closer," Dr Oyserman says. "If you see it as 'today' rather than on your calendar for sometime in the future, you're not going to put it off."

You need to create an unconscious sense of urgency, rather than an unconscious sense that you can put it off until tomorrow.

18 Look on the Bright Side

"Whether you think you can, or think you can't, you're right."
Henry Ford

The classic question to find out whether you're a pessimist or an optimist is whether you think your glass is half empty or half full.

Saying half empty and therefore being seen a pessimist would be regarded as the more negative of the two. But a characteristic most people would regard as negative doesn't have to be seen that way.

If you can find the silver lining, you can turn a negative into a positive and a pessimist into a realist.

Alexandra Wesnousky of New York University found in a study that more than 90% of people are inclined to see some sort of positive attribute associated with a typically negative trait.

She then decided to find out if seeing the positive in a negative might actually be beneficial.

> **If you can find the silver lining, you can turn a negative into a positive and a pessimist into a realist.**

The participants in the test took an impulsiveness survey. Afterwards, some participants were told they'd scored very high on the test, suggesting they were impulsive individuals, while others were told they'd scored very low.

Next the researchers led some of test participants to believe that impulsivity had a silver lining of making you more creative. These participants read a fake news article that cited scientific evidence to support the impulsive-creative connection. Other participants, meanwhile, read a fake news article refuting that link.

Finally, the test participants all completed an "alternative uses" task. A standard measure of creativity that asks people to list novel uses for common household items.

The results showed participants in the group who were told they were impulsive and who read about its "silver lining" scored higher on the creativity test than those who didn't.

So in a nutshell, telling people they were impulsive and that being impulsive was connected with being more creative, actually had the effect of making people more creative.

Of course this isn't really a hack you can do on yourself, but you could use it to help colleagues find the positive in a negative.

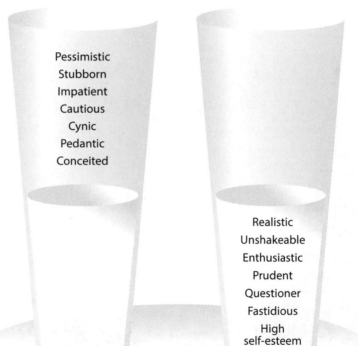

Pessimistic
Stubborn
Impatient
Cautious
Cynic
Pedantic
Conceited

Realistic
Unshakeable
Enthusiastic
Prudent
Questioner
Fastidious
High
self-esteem

People will perform much better when their negative traits are described using positive language.

PART 3

Problem Solving

Shortcuts to help your brain become better at solving problems

19 Take a Break

> "You can discover more about a person in an hour of play than in a year of conversation."
> *Plato*

Five days on, two days off. That's the work routine most people are used to. And for those two days off (commonly known as "the weekend") most off us try to switch off and not think about work.

It's vital to have time to switch off, especially if you've had a stressful week. But taking time off doesn't just have to be about switching off. It can be a great opportunity to come up with new and innovative ideas.

If we keep doing the same thing the neural pathways in our brain become neural superhighways. The more engrained they become, the harder it is to have fresh and original ideas.

But the brain is incredibly malleable, so if you can find new environments and influences, you'll soon start creating fresh neural pathways.

Working Holiday

Even highly creative people like the renowned graphic designer Stefan Sagmeister can feel like they are repeating themselves and that their work's getting stale. "Outwardly our last year with clients had been the most successful to date, we had won the most awards in our brief company history and the then booming economy had filled our coffers. But actually, I was bored. The work became repetitive," he said.

So in 2001 he decided to close his New York studio and take a year off. In fact he decided to repeat the exercise every seven years.

For the first sabbatical he stayed in New York. He looked through his diary and found all the things he said he'd really like to do if he hadn't been busy. He then made a list of these and ordered them into a weekly schedule.

In that year he rediscovered his love for his job. He also found that everything that he designed in the next seven years had its genesis from ideas he had on his sabbatical.

This meant that even though one of his initial fears had been that his clients might leave, they actually really appreciated the freshness the year off had brought to his work. So over the long term, the sabbatical had paid for itself.

Another person who strongly believed in the power of sabbaticals was Ferran Adrià, the owner and head chef of elBulli, voted best restaurant in the world for a record five times. He only opened elBulli for six months of the year. For the other six months it was closed so he and all the kitchen staff could experiment. "Now we will eat knowledge," as he likes to say.

At its height, elBulli could seat 8,000 customers a year, but had a waiting list of over two million. Even with that demand, Ferran wouldn't give up his experimentation time. Mind you, it was probably that time he spent experimenting and the resulting new culinary delights, that was the reason why his restaurant was so popular.

Stefan Sagmeister and Ferran Adrià were still working during the time they took off, but having the freedom of no customers to please and no meetings to attend, gave them the time to dream and think freely.

Of course, you don't need to takes months off to get the benefit of "free thinking" time.

3M have their 15% programme, which means all their staff have 15% of their week to work on their own projects. The idea for Post-It Notes famously came out of this time. Google have their 20% time, out of which Gmail, Google Maps, Google Talk and AdSense were born. AdSense alone is responsible for 25% of Google's annual revenue.

Taking time out not only re-shapes your mind, but also what you produce. It's an incredibly powerful tool that should never be underestimated.

66 Taking time out not only re-shapes your mind, but also what you produce. 99

Why not put a Post-It note above your desk? Not with anything on it, just a blank Post-It. You can use it as reminder of what you can do with a bit of free thinking time.

20 Just Start

> "The art of writing is the art of applying the seat of the pants to the seat of the chair."
> *Mary Heaton Vorse*

How many times have you heard someone say "I've got this great idea for a book/movie/business/product/app/website?" And how many of those people have actually gone ahead and done it?

People can no longer say there's no outlet for their ideas. Anyone can now self-publish, put a video on YouTube, start a website/blog, or get funding on Kickstarter for a product or business idea.

I think the big problem is fear of failure. And fear of failure is like nice dry kindling to the fire of procrastination.

The important thing is to start. It's all about learning on the job. Why do you think entrepreneurs always talk about "failing fast" and writers say, "writing is re-writing"?

Dr Piers Steel of the University of Calgary is probably the world's foremost expert on the subject of putting off until tomorrow what should be done today. In an article he wrote for The American Psychological Association[1] he said, "Essentially, procrastinators have less confidence in themselves, less expectancy that they can actually complete a task. … Perfectionism is not the culprit. In fact, perfectionists actually procrastinate less, but they worry about it more."

> **" Fear of failure is like nice dry kindling to the fire of procrastination. "**

The thing is no one gets it right first time, you learn by doing. What's most important is just to get started and not worry about whether what you're doing is good or bad. As Margaret Atwood said, "If I waited for perfection I would never have written a word."

A great way to force yourself to get started is with "morning pages". This is an exercise popularized by Julia Cameron in her book *The Artists Way*. Write two to three pages of handwritten, stream-of-consciousness writing, first thing in the morning.

The thing about the morning pages is they're not meant to be creative. They're more like morning therapy. Write about what's annoying you, your worries, your fears; just don't think too much about it. You don't even have to read them back and you certainly shouldn't show them to anyone else. It is like a warm-up before a race; no one judges an athlete on how good a warm-up he or she does before a race, but that doesn't mean it's any less essential.

By not really thinking about what you're writing, you're getting your unconscious involved. Our unconscious mind is a hugely powerful tool when it comes to coming up with ideas, but we need to get past our self-critical conscious thoughts to access it.

Another technique is to give yourself a deadline to come up with a certain amount of ideas for something. Whatever you're working on, try giving yourself 10 minutes to come up with 10 ideas on the subject. What's important is not to worry if these ideas are any good or not. Your only goal is to think of 10 ideas.

When you've got your 10 ideas, you may be surprised to find a few really interesting thoughts in amongst them. Like the morning pages, this exercise helps bypass your critical conscious mind and access your unconscious.

I'm sure you've been in a brainstorm where everyone starts to run out of ideas. Well, when this happens in one of my workshops, I get people to do this exercise. People who really feel they can't think of anything else, suddenly find a second wind.

Once you've done your morning pages or have come up with 10 ideas, working on your project of choice won't seem so daunting.

Don't expect perfection and just start.

If you could write 350 words a day (that's about two thirds of the amount of words in this chapter) and then do that five days a week (even tortured artists need a break at the weekend) for a year, you will have written 91,000 words.

There you go, you've written a first draft of a novel. You see, it wasn't that hard was it?

21 Take Away the Context

"It isn't that they can't see the solution. It is that they can't see the problem."

G.K. Chesterton

When we've got a problem to solve, our mind's tendency is to fixate on the common use of an object or its parts.

For example:

Problem 1: A ski company had a problem with their skis vibrating too much at high speeds.
Obvious action: Look at other manufacturers' skis and snowboards.

Problem 2: People feel a lift journey takes too long.
Obvious action: Make the lift faster.

Problem 3: Too many head injuries are happening in American football.
Obvious action: Give helmets more padding.

But in actual fact the best solution to these particular problems were found in some very unexpected areas:

> **Problem:** Vibrating skis   **Answer:** Violins
> **Problem:** Slow lifts   **Answer:** Mirrors
> **Problem:** Head injuries   **Answer:** Magnets.

Now you might think these very lateral solutions come from taking the blinkers off and widening your thinking. Wrong. You need to narrow your thinking. Reduce the problem to its purest form.

Take the problem of vibrating skis. The natural solution would be to focus on everything related to skiing: What happens to other makes of skis; what happens to snowboards; what happens on different types of snow at different speeds; what effect does the weight of the person on the skis have; and what effect does the width of the skis and the length of the skis have? And so on.

The trouble is everything is related to snow, skis and skiing. True, that's the arena of the problem, but that's not the problem.

The problem in its purest form is "vibration".

At high speeds, skis vibrated too much, lost contact with the snow and sent skiers out of control. What the ski company needed to do was reduce vibrations over 1,800 hertz.

They needed to forget about skiing and focus on whether there were any other areas where vibrations at over 1,800 hertz caused problems. That's when they found out that similar vibrations played havoc with violins, causing sound distortion. The violin designers solved this problem by using a metal grid. The ski company adapted this technology and the problem was solved.

Boil down Your Problem and Let It Simmer

Anthony McCaffrey a psychologist at the University of Massachusetts, has invented what he calls the "generic parts technique" or "GPT". It's all about boiling a problem down to its bare bones. People trained in GPT, McCaffrey's research suggests, solve problems such as this 67% more frequently than others.

For this GPT method to work, it's really important to not have any elements that might direct your thinking to a certain area.

"For each object in your problem, you break it into parts and ask two questions," explains McCaffrey, "1. Can it be broken down further? and 2. Does my description of the part imply a use?"

He gives this test as an example: Imagine you've been given two steel rings and told to make a "figure 8" out of them. Your tools are a candle and a box of matches.

Melted wax is sticky, but the wax isn't strong enough to hold the rings together. What about the other part of the candle? The wick. The trouble is the word "wick" implies a use. The whole purpose of a wick is to be set alight and when we hear the word "wick" that is all we think of.

"That tends to hinder people's ability to think of alternative uses for this part," says McCaffrey. Think of the wick more generically as a piece of string and you're liberated. Now you can remove the wick and tie the two rings together.

Tease Your Brain

This unconscious cognitive bias that we have to fight is what makes brainteasers hard. To put it to the test, here are a few for you to see if you can beat your cognitive bias at its own game.

1. A woman and her daughter walk into a restaurant. A man walks past and both women say "Hello father". How is this possible?

2. A man stands on one side of a river, his dog on the other. The man calls his dog. The dog immediately crosses the river without getting wet and without using a bridge or boat. How did the dog do it?

3. Two boxers are in a match scheduled for 12 rounds. One of the boxers gets knocked out after only six rounds, yet no man throws a punch. How is this possible?

4. A man turns off the light in his bedroom. The light switch is on the other side of the room from his bed, but he still manages to get into his bed before it is dark. How does he do it?

Answers:

4. He goes to bed when there is still daylight.

3. Both the boxers were women.

2. The river was frozen.

1. The man was a priest.

We're making assumptions without even realizing that we're doing it.

Now let's go back to the other two real life examples I gave earlier along with the vibrating skis.

The second problem of people feeling a lift journey took too long. This happened in the 1970s and the lift in question was in the Empire State Building. The obvious reaction to something taking too long was to make it faster. But these were state of the art lifts, so they couldn't be made to go any faster.

But if you take lifts out of the equation and you boil the problem down to "How do you make a journey go quicker?" Suddenly you're not thinking about lifts at all, but probably about car, plane or train journeys. You make those journeys feel like they go quicker by finding something to take your mind of the time it takes.

All people needed was a distraction. The solution they came up with was to put in floor-to-ceiling mirrors. This made the lifts feel more spacious as well as distracting people from any fear of falling and being in a confined space with strangers. Amazingly, in a survey after the mirrors had been installed, people commented on how much faster the lifts were, even though their speed hadn't actually changed at all.

The third problem was too many head injuries happening in American football. In our minds we see these players' helmets smashing together, so the obvious answer might be to add some sort of padding to soften the blow.

But the thing is, you're assuming that the players' helmets are still going to smash together. If you take away the problem of players' helmets smashing together, you're just left with "How do you stop two objects hitting each other?" Then it's not about softening the blow, but stopping the blow from happening in the first place.

Raymond Colello, a professor at the Virginia Commonwealth University School of Medicine, has had the idea of using magnets. When two players collide, the magnets in the helmets would repel each other. While the idea is still in development and there are various issues to be addressed, there's no denying it's certainly a non-obvious and fresh way to look at the problem.

So the next time you've got a problem to solve, try to boil it down to its purest form. Then try one of these techniques to help you come up with unbiased solutions. Just try typing your newly simplified problem into Google and you might find it gives you some interesting starting points in areas you'd never have expected.

> **The next time you've got a problem to solve, try to boil it down to its purest form.**

The other obvious idea is to get the thoughts of people who aren't aware of the original problem. State the problem with dry precision and make sure you avoid the opinion of anyone who might be biased like...YOU!

22 Keep Asking Why

"Curiosity is lying in wait for every secret."

Ralph Waldo Emerson

"Don't come to me with questions, come to me with solutions." Not the words of some impatient boss, but of your own mind. On second thoughts then, they are the words of an impatient boss.

Our brain has a lot on its plate, so it wants to solve problems quickly and get on to the next thing.

It was different when we were young. Our brains were full of questions it needed the answers to.

We ask about 40,000 questions between the ages of two and five. Four being our most inquisitive age when we ask about three hundred questions per day.

But these were questions we needed answers to in order to understand the world around us. Once children get older their questioning starts to tail off. A lot of people lay the blame on a school system that seems to value answers more than questions. I'm sure that's part of it, but I also think we don't need the answers as much.

From an evolutionary point of view our brains need just enough information to keep us safe and be able to function successfully in society. The answers to any other questions are just an added luxury.

But if you want to be a great problem solver, you need to cultivate a truly questioning mind.

> **If you want to be a great problem solver, you need to cultivate a truly questioning mind.**

You need that natural curiosity of a four-year-old, but you want to be asking the questions that have never been asked before.

Take Isaac Newton; he didn't have a to-do list, he had a why list.

When he was a student at Cambridge, he was uninterested in the set curriculum. At 19 he drew up a list of questions under 45 headings.

His aim was to constantly question the nature of matter, place, time, and motion.

He said he came up with the law of universal gravitation, "By thinking on it continually." It wasn't just because an apple hit him on the head.

Like Einstein who said, "I have no special talents. I am only passionately curious," he didn't believe he was a genius.

Newton's style was hard slog.

For example, he bought Descartes' Geometry and read it by himself. When he got through two or three pages and couldn't understand any further, he began again. He continued to do this until he truly understood what Descartes had to say on the subject.

It's the struggle to work things out that creates a great mind, not just having the answers.

I don't think we can just blame schools and society for making us less inquisitive. We need to create our own desire for how and why things happen.

Leonardo da Vinci even created a word for it: Curiosita – an insatiably curious approach to life and unrelenting quest for continuous learning. That's what made him such a great thinker, he wasn't just interested in one subject. He was a painter, but he was also a sculptor, architect, scientist, musician, mathematician, engineer, inventor, anatomist, geologist, astronomer, cartographer, botanist, historian and writer.

As well as being curious, it's also very important to cultivate a thoughtful mind instead of a quick one.

Darwin, like Einstein and Newton, relied upon perseverance and continual reflection, rather than memory and quick reflexes. "I have never been able to remember for more than a few days a single date or line of poetry." Instead, he had "the patience to reflect or ponder for any number of years over any unexplained problem. At no time am I a quick thinker or writer: whatever I have done in science has solely been by long pondering, patience, and industry."

In fact, if you look at Darwin's notebooks, you will see that he already had the information he needed to come up with his theory of evolution. He had all the jigsaw pieces; he just needed time to put them together.

Why, oh why, oh why?

Millions of people have been on walks in the countryside with their dogs and had to pick burrs out of their dogs' fur afterwards. But how many would have wondered why the burrs kept their stickiness.

It took the questioning mind of George de Mestral to ponder it and then put one of the burrs under a microscope and see hundreds of "hooks" that caught on anything with a loop, like curly hairs of a dog's coat. He then took this discovery and used it as the basis of his invention Velcro.

But having this questioning nature isn't just about discovering new ideas; it's also a way of questioning something that already exists, that isn't working.

Ricardo Semler, CEO of Brazilian company Semco, famous for its radical industrial democracy, suggests that one way to get to a greater wisdom is to simply ask three "Whys?" in a row about everything you are doing.

He says, "The first 'Why?' you always have a good answer for. Then the second 'Why?' starts getting difficult to answer. By the third 'Why?' you realize that, in fact, you really don't know why you're doing what you're doing." Semler says that by asking "Why?" three times, you start to get clearer about who you are and why you are here.

Here's an example of how the "three whys" get to the heart of the problem:

Q: Why can't more people in our company work from home?

A: Because we don't know if we can trust them to work a full day.

Q: Why are we employing people who we can't trust?

A: We do trust them, when they are in the office.

Q: Why are we treating our staff like children?

A: Erm…

With an inquiring mind you don't know where you're going or what the future holds. But what you do know is that when you get there it'll be a lot more interesting.

23 Sleep Well

> "Sleeping is no mean art: for its sake one must stay awake all day."
> *Friedrich Nietzsche*

This is the most important of all brainhacks.

Sleep.

Sleep offers so many benefits. A lot of the time we think if we're busy we can get by on less sleep and extra caffeine. But if you want your brain to function better and to be more productive, sweet dreams will always beat a strong coffee.

Now I'm sure you've experienced those annoying people who say they can function just as well on four hours of sleep as you can on seven or eight.

Well, they're right and they're wrong. Studies have found that a sleep-deprived person can in fact deliver exactly the same results in any exercise as someone who isn't sleep deprived.

The problem comes when you lose focus. Whether we are sleep deprived or not, we're all going to lose focus at certain times.

> **" Sweet dreams will always beat a strong coffee. "**

Dr Clifford Saper, of Harvard University, said: "The brain of the sleep-deprived individual is working normally sometimes, but intermittently suffers from something akin to power failure."[1]

If you've had a good night's sleep and you lose focus, your brain can compensate for that by increasing attention. But for anyone who is sleep deprived, they haven't got the brainpower to steer themselves back to being focused.

What's even worse, sleep-deprived people don't realize their performance has decreased.

Professor Michael Chee, the lead researcher at Harvard, said: "The periods of apparently normal functioning could give a false sense of competency and security when, in fact, the brain's inconsistency could have dire consequences."[2]

The A to Zzzzzzz of Sleep

A good night's sleep returns your brain to full power. Creativity, ingenuity, confidence, leadership, and decision-making can all be enhanced simply by getting enough sleep.

But it's not just lack of sleep that can have a negative effect on us. Oversleeping can be bad for us as well. Regularly having more than nine hours of sleep a night or having less than five hours of sleep a night can both be really bad for you. Both markedly increasing your chance of cardiovascular disease like heart attacks, strokes and angina attacks.

Dr Jane Ferrie, who led the study of 30,000 adults for University College London, said the decline in brain function suffered by people who got too much or too little sleep was equivalent to them having aged between four and seven years.

❝ A good night's sleep returns your brain to full power. ❞

It also seems the optimum amount of sleep we should have a night isn't eight hours, but seven. In fact even one hour more or less than seven hours increased the likelihood of heart disease, the study found.

But don't worry, this doesn't mean your Sunday morning lie-in should carry a health warning.

The dangers associated with sleeping too long only affects you when it happens over a long period. If you've had a really busy week at work of early mornings and late nights (or if you have children), then a lie in is vital.

Dr David Dinges from the University of Pennsylvania said: "The additional hour or two of sleep in the morning after a period of chronic partial sleep loss has genuine benefits for continued recovery of behavioural alertness."[3]

A single, proper lie-in can be all that is required to replenish the brain and boost energy, alertness and attention span after a week of restricted sleep.

The Nap Zone. Time to Hit Snooze.

There's also a reason why you hit that dip after lunch. It's your body trying to tell you something. If you used your circadian biological clock to tell the time you'd know you're strongest sleep drive generally occurs between 2:00–4:00 a.m. at night and in the afternoon between 1:00–3:00 p.m.

We desperately try to fight it with double espressos, but your body and more importantly your brain, is telling you, it wants and needs, some shut-eye.

Our obsession with one long sleep has only been adopted since the industrial revolution. Before then most people would take naps. People used to have day beds in their living rooms and they were called day beds for a reason.

Of course many countries like Spain and India do stop for afternoon rests. In China, many companies encourage workers to take an hour's nap after lunch. Japan is also changing its workaholic ways and persuading its workers to take naps. They've even got nap cafes popping up where you can buy a snooze.

Sleep experts have found that daytime naps can improve many things. It can increase alertness, boost creativity, reduce stress, improve perception, stamina, motor skills and accuracy, brighten your mood and boost memory.

Taking a nap also helps in solidifying memories. When a memory is first recorded in the hippocampus (the area in the brain that converts short-term into long-term memory), it's still fragile and can be easily forgotten. Napping, it seems, pushes memories to the neocortex, the brain's more permanent storage, preventing them from being "overwritten". Sleep is a necessary process that clears the brain's short-term memory storage so there is room to absorb new information.

The lead researcher from the University of California, Berkeley, Dr Matthew Walker, says, "Sleep prepares the brain like a dry sponge, ready to soak up new information."[4]

A reason, no doubt, why Leonardo da Vinci, Napoleon, Thomas Edison, Eleanor Roosevelt, President John F. Kennedy and Winston Churchill swore by them.

10, 20 or 40 Winks?

So if you're on board with the whole nap idea, how do you fit one in? It's easy if you work at a company like Google and you have nap pods, but for everyone else it's a bit harder.

Firstly, you don't need to nap for long to feel the benefit. In a study by Professor Leon Lack from Flinders University in Adelaide, it was found that 10 to 15 minutes seems to be the optimum period in terms of improving mental operations. And that improvement in performance and alertness seems to be maintained for up to two and sometimes three hours after the nap.

However, the five-minute nap wasn't long enough to create any benefit, and longer naps of 25 to 30 minutes led to the subjects being somewhat drowsy and less alert for up to an hour after the nap.

Now all you need to do is find a place to have a nap. If you feel uncomfortable putting your head down at your desk, try to find an empty meeting room, or if you've got a park nearby, try sitting under a tree. If you really can't find anywhere, you can always sit on the toilet for ten minutes.

> ❝ **You don't need to nap for long to feel the benefit.** ❞

And instead of having a coffee at the end of your lunch break, why not try having a nap instead?

You could even bring the subject up at work as a way to improve productivity. But if you are thinking of organizing a meeting about it, don't arrange it for three o'clock!

24 Be More Sarcastic

"Sarcasm is the lowest form of wit."

Oscar Wilde

The trouble with the quote above is, that it's only part of the quote. What Oscar Wilde actually said was, "Sarcasm is the lowest form of wit but the highest form of intelligence." And as a pretty sarcastic man himself, I think maybe the first part of the quote was meant sarcastically.

But for me the interesting part of the quote is that it's "the highest form of intelligence", because understanding sarcasm actually requires many processes in the brain.

An Israeli team led by Dr Simone Shamay-Tsoory at the Haifa University compared healthy people alongside people with damaged brains and found that damage to the prefrontal lobes at the front of the brain can stop you understanding sarcasm.

She said this fitted with what is already known about the anatomy of the brain. Language areas on the left hand side of the brain interpret the literal meaning of words and the frontal lobes and the right side of the brain understand the social and emotional context.

The reason that sarcasm requires all these different parts of the brain is what makes it a powerful tool. Because being sarcastic and also listening to someone being sarcastic actually makes you more creative, according to the study published in *Organizational Behavior and Human Decision Processes* journal.

> ❝ Being sarcastic and also listening to someone being sarcastic actually makes you more creative. ❞

A team of researchers from Insead Business School, and Harvard and Columbia universities, led by Dr Li Huang, carried out a number of studies involving more than 300 men and women. Each was designed to test the effects on subsequent creativity after making and receiving sarcastic comments.

One of the main experiments involved people being exposed to sarcastic or sincere comments and then faced with a psychological test involving creativity.

The results showed that sarcasm had a huge impact on the participants' ability to solve the problem. Of those who had been the butt of sarcastic comments, 75% came up with the right solution, compared with only 25% who had been exposed to sincere comments. Some 64% of those who *made* sarcastic comments were correct too, compared with 30% of a control group.

That's double the performance for people making sarcastic comments and treble for people on the receiving end. Being on the receiving end is no doubt higher because working out what's sarcastic uses more of the brain than simply being sarcastic.

Understanding sarcasm requires comprehending contradictory statements, for example "Don't work too hard" said to someone who is clearly resting. This puts the brain into abstract thinking mode, and the researchers said that there is decades of work to show that abstract thinking increases creativity.

"We have shown that creativity is enhanced following all types of sarcasm, from sarcastic anger and criticism to sarcastic compliments and banter," the researchers said. "All forms of sarcastic exchanges, not just sarcastic anger or criticism, seem to exercise the brain more."

Health and Safety

The trouble is sarcasm is often to used to convey thinly disguised disapproval, contempt and scorn. Even if it makes you more creative, these aren't very productive and helpful emotions to have at work.

One of the researchers, Francesca Gino, said: "Our research proposed and has shown that to minimize the relational cost while still benefiting creatively, sarcasm is better used between people who have a trusting relationship."

If it's amongst work colleagues and friends with whom you have a good relationship, then it's a healthy way to put your brain into abstract thinking mode and make you more creative. But if it's contemptuous or angry sarcasm, the negative emotions it creates outweigh the creative benefits.

Here are a few examples:

Contempt

Boss to Employee:

> "Good news, you're going to have to work this weekend."

Resentment

Boss:

> "We're really behind with the project, would you be able to work the weekend?"

Employee:

> "Of course, I'd be happy to, I didn't really want to see any of my friends anyway."

Friendly banter

One colleague to another:

> "Congratulations, I hear you've got the opportunity to be in work all weekend. I'm really happy for you."

Using sarcasm to purposely make people feel uncomfortable is definitely the lowest form of wit. Using sarcasm to tell a colleague in an unpatronizing way that you understand their plight, knowing that it'll also make you both more creative, is the highest form of intelligence.

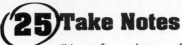
(25) Take Notes

"Very often, gleams of light come in a few minutes' sleeplessness, in a second perhaps; you must fix them. To entrust them to the relaxed brain is like writing on water; there is every chance that on the morrow there will be no slightest trace left of any happening."

Antonin Sertillanges

Have you had that feeling of having a great idea and then not being able to remember it later in the day? It's incredibly frustrating.

The idea that was going to make you millions, save the world, inspire a nation…is gone.

Our thought process is very fluid and our thoughts often ephemeral. So don't leave it for even ten minutes, write it down! It may not seem as elegant as it did in your head. It may not be fully formed. Don't worry; just make a note of it.

66 *Don't leave it for even ten minutes, write it down!* 99

Whenever Woody Allen has an idea, he writes it down on a piece of paper and puts it in a drawer in his bedside table. When he's finished one film and it's time to write another, he takes all the scraps of paper from the drawer and spreads them out on his bed. He then goes through them one by one and sees if any of them spark anything off.

They can be as simple as one line. This is one of them: "A man inherits all the magic tricks of a great magician."[1] As he looks at each one he thinks if there's anything about it that inspires him. If there's nothing, he puts it back in the drawer and moves on to the next one.

I think what's interesting is that if he doesn't find an idea inspiring he doesn't chuck it out; he puts it back in the drawer. Six months or a year later he could have read something or have seen something that would suddenly make one of the ideas that he previously rejected, spring to life.

That's why it's so important to keep a record of your thoughts. You don't know when the other pieces of the jigsaw are going to turn up.

> 66 *You don't know when the other pieces of the jigsaw are going to turn up.* 99

One of the other benefits of writing things down is you're not just making a record of it on paper, but also in your long-term memory, the mind's filing system. Once firmly lodged in your mind, your unconscious can start working on developing the idea.

The danger comes when we're suffering from information overload from the Internet. A lot of what we read online just stays in our "working memory", the temporary storage area for ideas. And this temporary storage area can only take so much information.

Every time we shift our attention, the brain has to reorient itself, further taxing our mental resources. Many studies have shown that switching between just two tasks can add substantially to our cognitive load. And that's what we do a lot while we're online. Flitting from one story to the next, following links, checking email and social media.

Even just reading an online article still creates more cognitive load than reading it in print. There are the distractions of links on the same page as well as the ones within the article. Even if you don't click on the links in the article, you have still had to make the choice not to click on it and that in itself is distracting.

So how do you remember all the interesting things you read online? The obvious thing is just to bookmark the page. The trouble is, we get into the habit of just reading the title and then bookmarking the page to read later, which, of course, we never end up doing.

My advice is to take a leaf out of the book of another group of people suffering from information overload – the renaissance scholars. And the book you should take a leaf out of is what they called their commonplace books.

The commonplace book wasn't a diary; it was a way to compile knowledge. They were filled with items of every kind: medical, recipes, quotations, letters, poems, ideas, speeches and proverbs. Three hundred years ago they weren't reading books from cover to cover, they were dipping into them for useful information and then writing down whatever they found of interest in their commonplace book. So in a way, it wasn't really that different from how we browse the Internet now. The big difference is how they kept a record of what they found interesting. They wrote it down.

So if you really want the best way to retain information from the Internet you should write it down. Obviously this requires a lot of work. If you haven't got time for this, cut and paste whatever you find of interest online into your own digital commonplace book.

If you don't keep digital clippings, the interesting stories you read will be bundled in with everything else you're bombarded with online and will be thrown out by your overloaded temporary memory. Surf and turf!

So wherever or whenever, if you have a thought or an idea, give that little spark a chance of greatness and write it down.

> **" Give that little spark a chance of greatness and write it down. "**

26 Notice Your Mistakes

"Success does not consist in never making mistakes but in never making the same one a second time."

George Bernard Shaw

How do you feel when you get an email that has a spelling mistake in it?

I know when I get one, I feel like the person sending me the email has written it in a rush. It makes me think they don't see it as important because they haven't checked it through properly.

The thing is, I know I send emails with mistakes in them as well. The problem isn't always that we haven't checked it through, it's that we can't see the mistakes.

You may very well have seen this test before, but if not, try reading through the next paragraph:

Aoccdrnig to rsecearh at Cmabrigde Uinervtisy, it deosn't mttaer in waht oredr the ltteers in a wrod are, the olny iprmoatnt tihng is taht the frist and lsat ltteer be at the rghit pclae. The rset can be a toatl mses and you can sitll raed it wouthit a porbelm. Tihs is bcuseae the huamn mnid deos not raed ervey lteter by istlef, but the wrod as a wlohe.

It's incredible really, but as you've just read, it's because our mind reads the whole word and not every letter. Give it to a five or six-year-old to read and they'd probably have the same reaction as my spellcheck had: total meltdown. When children are starting to read, they are reading each letter in the word, so to them it looks like complete gobbledygook. This is because the word patterns in their brains have not yet become rigid.

Our word patterns are so rigid that once we read the scrambled letters as words, we no longer see them as a bunch of mixed up letters but as ordinary words.

The purpose of these rigid patterns is so that we don't have to read every letter and can get the message quicker. What's important to us is what is written, not how it's written.

The trouble with pattern recognition systems is that they're a shortcut, so it makes it harder for us to see our mistakes.

Try this test. Don't think about it too much. Just say the answers to yourself in your head:

Q: What's a common abbreviation for Coca-Cola?

Q: What do we call the sound a frog makes?

Q: What is a comedian's funny story called?

Q: What do you call the white of an egg?

Did you answer "yolk"? If you did, that's because of the mind's liking for solving problems by creating patterns. It's just trying to save you time, but it's being a bit too clever for it's own good. Because you answer them quickly you're not really thinking about the answers, so your unconscious takes over. It sees that the first three answers (Coke, croak, joke) all ended in the same sound, so when you get to the question about the white of an egg, it thinks what part of the egg ends in a "K" sound, oh yeah, "yolk!".

Of course, if you think about it you know the real answer, but if you answer quickly, your unconscious takes over and looks for patterns. Obviously the whole point of pattern recognition is to enable us to simplify and cope with a complex world, but as you've just seen, it's not perfect. Perhaps as humans we're still in the beta testing phase.

Here's another example:

After reading the

the sentence, you are

now aware that the

the human brain

often does not

inform you that the

the word 'the' has

been repeated

twice every time.

Your mind is reading it for what it means, not for the actual separate words. And of course, that's the important thing. But not if you're checking an email, blog or document for mistakes.

The trouble is when we're proofreading our own work, we have to compete with the version that's already in our heads. So however hard we try, we read for meaning, so we end up not seeing our mistakes. When there's a problem with the meaning our brain will pick up on it, but if it's just a misspelt word, it's a lot harder.

Obviously, whoever reads what you've written has the same unconscious patterning, which is why the previous exercises work for everybody. But the big benefit they have, is that they are reading it for the first time, trying to discover its meaning – they don't have a version of it in their heads like you do.

So that's your first port of call: get someone else to read it before you send it off. This is fine for a document or blog, but you can't ask someone to read every email you send.

> ❝ When there's a problem with the meaning, our brain will pick up on it, but if it's just a misspelt word it's a lot harder. ❞

When you're proofreading your own work, the secret is to make yourself as unfamiliar with your work as possible. Try changing the colour of the type and the typeface itself. Even making the type smaller than normal, or much bigger. The whole point is not to make it an easy read for yourself, and in that way you're more likely to notice small mistakes.

If you're not sure about the content of what you've written, especially if it's a longer length project like a book, don't read it back straight away. Put it in a drawer for a couple of weeks, then hopefully when you do read it, the memory of it won't be as vivid. This will help it seem fresher on the page. As the writer, Neil Gaiman, says about his first drafts: "Put it away, and come back to it after you are well into another project. Otherwise, you will never see the mistakes you have made – but everyone else will."

27 Write by Hand

"Men have become the tools of their tools."
Henry David Thoreau

Imagine ten years from now, it could be quite feasible that children wouldn't be taught handwriting at school and would just learn to type.

Would that be such a bad thing?

Yes, it would.

You might argue that typing is better, because it's easier to do and easier to read. But the reason that handwriting is harder is exactly why it's so important.

As most people can type significantly faster than they can write, it's like taking verbatim notes. But the trouble is, you're not being forced to think about what you write.

When you take notes by hand you can't write everything down. This means you have to think about the "essence" of what's being said.

Writing by hand actually uses more of the brain, as you need to make several strokes for each letter. Your working memory gets activated, as well as brain areas used for thinking and language. On a keyboard, one tap creates an entire letter, so your relationship with making the letter is shorter and more superficial.

The more areas of the brain that are firing, the stronger connection is between the content of what you're writing and your brain; therefore the more you'll be able to remember later on.

Now you might argue that surely it's better to take more comprehensive typewritten notes at a meeting, conference or lecture and then review and distill them at your leisure. But research has proved otherwise.

The Pen Is Mightier Than the Keyboard

Research by Pam Mueller of Princeton and Daniel Oppenheimer of UCLA has shown that students who write their notes on paper actually learn more.

Across three experiments, Mueller and Oppenheimer had students take notes in a classroom setting. They then tested students on their memory for factual detail, their conceptual understanding of the material, and their ability to synthesize and generalize the information.

Half of the students were instructed to take notes with a laptop, and the other half to write out their notes by hand. As expected, the students who used laptops took more notes, but in each study, those who wrote out their notes by hand had a stronger conceptual understanding of the subject they'd listened to. They were also found to be more successful in applying and integrating the material compared to those who took notes with their laptops.

Even when the students were given the chance to study their notes for a test a week later, those who took longhand notes still outperformed laptop note takers.

And to prove it's better to take handwritten notes whatever the subject, the lectures covered a varied range of topics from faith, respiration and economics, to algorithms, bread and bats.

So if you are ever in need of information about the lesser dog-faced fruit bat, there will be a Princeton student who writes notes by hand who will be able to help you.

When you type notes you are writing down what is being said. When you are hand writing notes you are re-writing. It forces the brain to engage more and therefore creates a stronger memory of the subject matter.

Because longhand notes contain your own words and handwriting, they may serve as more effective memory cues by recreating the context (thought processes, emotions, conclusions) as well as content (individual facts).

The other huge benefit of taking handwritten notes is that you can't be distracted by the lure of the Internet. It has been found that students using laptops spend as much as 40% of their time using applications unrelated to their course work.

Just because something's faster, it doesn't necessarily mean it's better. As with all things brain-related, the more you engage it, the better the results.

PART 4

Idea Generation

How to come up with more and better ideas

28 Map It Out

"Learning how to learn is life's most important skill."
Tony Buzan

The mind map is a great brainhacking tool because it works by association in the same way the brain does. But that's not what this Brainhack is about. This is about is how to make them an even more powerful tool than they already are.

Tony Buzan invented the term "mind map" in the 1970s to describe the graphical technique for visualizing connections between ideas or information. At that time the only way to use one was to draw it out on paper. Now however, there is a proliferation of mind mapping apps.

These digital mind maps have the benefit of being able to be bigger and more versatile – you can have links and attach files. But there's one big disadvantage: they don't engage the brain in the same way.

I've already mentioned in the last chapter that you remember things better when you write them down, and also engage more parts of the brain. But that's just one of the reasons why a hand-drawn mind map is better.

Our brains are also naturally more engaged by mind maps that are drawn. Just do a search on Google for mind maps and see which ones you are most attracted to. I'm sure you'll also find that they're the ones that use lots of different colours and images.

Annett Schmeck from the University of Duisburg-Essen found that we learn better when we create drawings as part of our notes.

She gave schoolchildren an 850-word passage about the biology of influenza, broken down into seven paragraphs. This was an unfamiliar topic to them, and they knew they were going to be tested on the content afterwards.

Half the pupils were asked to produce a drawing to accompany each of the paragraphs of the text; the other half only had the text itself to study.

In a multiple choice test afterwards the children who used drawings to aid their learning scored an average of 61%. The pupils who only studied the text scored an average of just 44%.

In further tests, pupils were given pictures to accompany the text. But even then, they still didn't score as highly as the schoolchildren who drew their own pictures.

They also found that the children who took most care over their drawings, also got the best scores.

Using colours is also an important tool to make mind maps more powerful. It doesn't just make it look prettier; like drawings, it helps you remember the information better.

The richer the memory of it, the more we'll think about it and the more useful the map will be in helping us find a solution to a problem.

Michael Tipper, an experienced consultant on mind mapping, says: "Separating branches of your map by colour stimulates the creative side of your brain, helps you visually separate and recall distinct themes of the stuff you're working through, and encourages you to map through even boring topics that seem cut-and-dry."

Colours help create further delineation on your map and are another tool to help embed the information in your memory. By associating something with a colour as well the title of the group it's in, you are remembering it twice. You are using two different parts of the brain, the one that deals with colour association and the one that deals with language.

29 Run a Brain Marathon

"A collection of a hundred Great Brains makes one big fathead."
Carl Jung

There are lots of problems with brainstorms, but the main one is they don't go on for long enough.

They usually stop when people have run out of ideas and you get those embarrassing silences. But those embarrassing silences are when your unconscious starts engaging on the problem and is a vital part to coming up with great ideas.

> **❝ There are lots of problems with brainstorms, but the main one is they don't go on for long enough. ❞**

The way brainstorms are practised in most companies today is still almost exactly the same way that was recommended by their inventor, advertising executive Alex Osborn. But he invented it in 1953, over sixty years ago. Business and our understanding of how the brain works has moved on so much in that time and yet we're still hanging onto this old technique for so many of our idea gathering sessions.

The fact is, brainstorms do have a useful part to play in solving problems. They can be very useful at the start and the end of the process. The trouble is a lot of the time they're used as the *only* part of the process.

Here are some of the problems with a brainstorm:

- The more extrovert characters often dominate the session.
- Early ideas tend to have a disproportionate influence over the direction the whole session takes.
- You listen and focus on other people's ideas and don't spend time thinking about your own. When we hear someone else's solution, it's like a magnet and it pulls our focus towards it.
- After the idea generation process, the decision makers often tend to choose the moderately creative over the highly creative ideas.

Some of these problems can be solved by a technique called brainwriting. This is where people either write their ideas down before or at the start of the session. They then stick them all up on the wall anonymously.

This is definitely a way to improve brainstorms. But the decision makers can still use the session to pick a solution to the problem, rather than using the ideas as starting points for further thought.

Too many people in a group can also be a problem. When you get embarrassing silences with a group of fifteen people you wrap up the session. But when there are two, three or four of you, you can ride the silence.

In Alex Osborn's 1953 book *Applied Imagination* he introduced the concept of the brainstorm because he claimed that brainstorming was more effective in generating ideas than individuals working alone.

But around the same time Bill Bernbach, of advertising agency DDB, also introduced the idea of a team of people working together to solve ideas. It's just that his idea of the "creative team" involved only two people. And they wouldn't just try to come up with ideas in one-hour times slots, but day in, day out.

Sometimes these creative teams involve more than two people as in American TV's "writers rooms". But what all these creative team sessions have in common is what brainstorms don't: time, a trusting environment, a lack of ego and drive to keep working on the problem.

Two of the writers of the critically acclaimed TV series *Breaking Bad*, Thomas Schnauz and Peter Gould, were interviewed by NPR's *Fresh Air* and gave a few insights into how they worked.

They said that if you feel like you're going to be criticized for something you say, then you're not going to say it. It's really important to be in an environment where you would feel comfortable saying the stupidest of things, because often good ideas would arise from these.

Instead of trying to negate what another person says, they believe you should try to build on it. And as you build on each thought, you come up with a run of thoughts. Sometimes something great comes out of it and sometimes it doesn't lead anywhere and you move on. But what is important is you've investigated its potential. "It's a really sophisticated form of play", said Peter.

> ## Instead of trying to negate what another person says, you should try and build on it. "

I think the brainstorm has become the dominant model for problem solving in business, because it's easy and quick. You get everyone together for an hour, throw ideas around and then the boss picks his favourite. You know at the end of the hour you'll have some solutions to your problem and you can give it a big tick and move on.

But it's unlikely that the brainstorm has created the best solution. If you genuinely want good ideas, borrow the model from creative teams whose job it is to come up with ideas on a daily basis.

After all, if you want to know how to grow flowers, you wouldn't ask a florist, you'd ask a gardener.

If you want to get good ideas you've got to work at it. It can be fun and it can be frustrating, but you've got to put in the hours.

> ## If you want to get good ideas you've got to work at it. "

So here's the model I would suggest instead of the brainstorm.

THE
BRAIN MARATHON

1. **Make sure the signpost is pointing in the right direction:**
   Really understanding the problem you're trying to solve is vital to creating a good solution. This is where a brainstorm can be useful. It can feed in as much background information as possible. Techniques in Brainhacks 21 Take Away The Context, 22 Keep Asking Why and 28 Map It Out, can be really useful at this stage.

Think, think, think
Get people into small teams of two, three or four and then allocate a decent block of time for them to work on the problem. The very minimum should be a whole morning or afternoon.

If you can get out of the office, that's even better. "Lots of the best ideas occur when camaraderie and chemistry have built up between employees, and breaks from the office together – even for just a day – can make all the difference," says Richard Branson.[1]

After an initial outpouring of ideas you'll find yourself drying up. This is the stage when brainstorms usually stop. But don't think it's any reflection on your thinking abilities. It happens to all creative thinkers.

That point when you get stuck and feel like you're not getting anywhere, that's when you're hacking your brain and getting your unconscious and its huge processing power involved. What's important is to stay together and don't drift back to your desks to check emails.

 Decision Time
Once you've spent the morning working on a problem, have a break from it and then get back together for an hour at the end of the day to review your ideas.

This is when you need to narrow down your ideas and pick your favourites. Instead of your boss picking from a longlist in a brainstorm, you get to narrow down the choice to a shortlist. The benefit of this is you get to argue out amongst yourselves the benefit of one idea over another and in doing so create a solid argument for each idea.

Brainstorms might come in convenient half hour and hour time slots, but ideas don't. So if you're really serious about finding a solution to a problem, give the brain marathon a try.

30 Do Something Different

"If all you own is a hammer, everything looks like a nail."
Abraham Maslow

If asked whether it is better to have more knowledge of a subject than less, most people's natural inclination would be to say more. It's why we have the phrase "A little knowledge is a dangerous thing". The implication being, with a little knowledge you can be misled into thinking you're an expert on a subject.

But knowledge is often just other people's ideas and is often seen as set in stone. If you want to look at something in a fresh way you need to break away from existing ideas on a subject.

I think that's why Einstein tweaked it to: "A little knowledge is a dangerous thing. So is a lot."

It's no surprise then that Einstein himself had what was called his "miracle year" (or his miracle "three and a half months" to be more precise), when he was just twenty-six. In that time, he wrote three papers, one of which won him the Nobel prize, one that confirmed beyond doubt the existence and size of atoms, and another that introduced the mind, space and time-bending concept of special relativity.

Although he took a teaching diploma at Zurich Polytechnic, he never went to university and so was not influenced by the ideas and theories of "learned" professors. At the time he was working in the patent office in Bern and was doing science on the side.

> **Once we see something in a certain light or used for a certain purpose, it's very hard to see it in a different way.**

Once we have a certain amount of knowledge on a subject we can start to suffer from "functional fixedness" or "stuck in a rut" syndrome. It basically means that once we see something in a certain light or used for a certain purpose, it's very hard to see it in a different way.

A good example of breaking out of functional fixedness is Harry Beck's London Underground map. Until 1933, all the Underground maps had been geographically correct.

But that was all about to change. While working as an electrical engineering draftsman at the London Underground Signals Office, Harry Beck came up with a revolutionary design that disobeyed all conventional mapping rules. It was initially rejected by the London Transport publicity office for being too radical, but was given a small trial and was taken up after the public fell in love with it.

As Beck himself said, "If you're going underground, why do you need to bother about geography?"

Undoubtedly influenced by electrical circuit boards, he wasn't constrained by the "knowledge" that maps have to be geographically correct.

The term "functional fixedness" was coined by Karl Duncker and relates to a mental block against using an object in a new way.

He demonstrated this with his "candle problem". He gave the participants a candle, a box of drawing pins, and a book of matches, and asked them to attach the candle to the wall so that it did not drip wax onto the table below.

Duncker found that participants tried to attach the candle directly to the wall with the tacks, or glue it to the wall by melting it. Very few of them thought of using the inside of the box as a candleholder and pinning this to the wall.

The participants were "fixated" on the box's normal function of holding drawing pins and couldn't imagine it as a candleholder. Forget thinking outside the box, they couldn't even think of it as a box! Interestingly, when the participants were presented with an empty drawing pin box, they were twice as likely to solve the problem.

Of course, functional fixedness doesn't just relate to objects. It can affect concepts and services as well.

I was running a workshop for a large multinational company, which wanted to come up with solutions to how its departments in America and England could interact better given the time difference. The workshop was in London but there was a mix of people from the English and American offices.

Everyone thought about the problem for a bit and then stuck their ideas on the wall. As everyone looked over the ideas, I noticed there was one in particular that was making everyone laugh.

I went over and had a look and it simply said, "The Americans should get up really early." When I asked which ideas people thought had potential no one mentioned this one. It was seen a joke. I'm sure even the person who wrote it didn't expect it to be considered seriously.

They were all so engrained in the belief that a standard office workday is 9 to 5, that they didn't even consider it a viable option. But imagine if the Americans started at 6:00 a.m. If you take out the hour allocated for lunch, they could actually finish at 1:00 p.m. every day and have the afternoon off. Suddenly it's not a joke any more but has become quite an attractive option.

We're so set in thinking of things in a certain way. It's why, when a simple new idea comes along you often hear, "That's so obvious; why hasn't anyone thought of that before?" They haven't thought of it before because everyone is so fixed in their thinking.

A good example of this is the upside-down ketchup bottle. Why did it take so long to invent? I think it's just because we're fixed into this view that the bottle top should always be at the top. The fact that the lid is also called a "top" doesn't help either. It's an unconscious double whammy. Functional fixedness with a side order of cognitive bias.

So what's the answer? Well, first and foremost, to create more neural pathways in your brain. When you've got a problem and you've got a choice of four different paths to take instead of one, you're far more likely to go somewhere new with it.

To Think Different, Do Different

What's interesting is that doing anything new will help you break out of functionally fixed thinking.

It's not the relevance that matters; it's the newness.

Dutch psychologist Dr Simone Ritter from Radboud University Nijmegen wanted to prove this so she devised two tests.

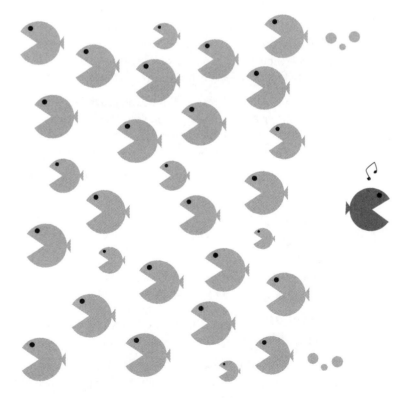

In the first test, participants put on virtual reality headsets and took a three-minute stroll through a virtual version of the university cafeteria where illogical things happened. For instance, when participants walked up to a suitcase standing on a table, the size of the suitcase decreased, but as they walked away, it increased.

She also created another test in the real cafeteria. A classic Dutch breakfast believe it or not, is bread and butter with chocolate sprinkles on top. As you'd expect, the standard way to prepare it is to butter the bread and then sprinkle on the chocolate.

But what Dr Ritter did was to get the participants to put the chocolate sprinkles on a plate and then place the buttered bread, butter side down onto the sprinkles. They still ended up with bread and butter with chocolate sprinkles; it's just that the method they used to get there was very unorthodox.

After doing both tests, the participants were given classic creativity tests like: How many different uses can you think of for a household brick? It was found that their levels of creativity had risen by as much as 15%.

What they also found was it worked because it was an active experience. When people were shown a film of the strange things that happened in the virtual cafe there was no increase in their levels of creativity. They needed to actually experience it for themselves for it to make a difference.

It's all about seeking out that little unconscious jolt of surprise that a new perspective can give you.

> **❝ It's all about seeking out that little unconscious jolt of surprise that a new perspective can give you. ❞**

There are many ways to get this change of perspective jolt from experiencing something everyday in a different way.

An interesting example of this is from New Yorker Alexandra Horowitz's book, *On Looking*. She went on eleven walks around her block with a different companion each time.

She wanted to see this very familiar walk which she did every day, through different eyes. Each one transformed the familiar surroundings and helped her see it in a fresh and interesting new way.

A sound engineer transformed the urban noise into the characteristic, flavourful clatter of the city. Each sound felt invited, a pleasure. A typographer helped her to stop reading signs and look at them instead. The linguistic part of her brain rested and the shape-identifying part hummed with activity. Through a geologist's eyes, the city suddenly became not a sterile "man-made" object but a thriving ecosystem of living and once-living landscape.

By changing your focus the ordinary can become extraordinary again.

But don't feel you have to wait till you get outside the office. Dr Ritter says, "Start a brainstorming session with something unexpected and you'll find that it is easier for participants to think outside the box."

If you want your neurons to make new connections, you need to connect with the world in a new way.

> **"If you want your neurons to make new connections, you need to connect with the world in a new way."**

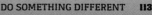

31 Don't Try to Have Good Ideas

"Nothing is more dangerous than an idea when it is the only one you have."

Émile Chartier

The first rule of having good ideas: Don't try to have good ideas.

What's important is just to have ideas. When you have an idea you don't know how good it is. It can only be judged when you have more ideas to compare it to.

Author and entrepreneur Seth Godin said "Someone asked me where I get all my good ideas, explaining that it takes him a month or two to come up with one and I seem to have more than that. I asked him how many bad ideas he has every month. He paused and said, 'None.'"

When there's pressure to think of a "great" idea, you start judging your ideas before you've even written them down.

> ❝ **The first rule of having good ideas: Don't try to have good ideas.** ❞

American advertising legend George Lois said that he told everyone in his department to come up with a great idea for a client. He came back in an hour and nobody had any ideas at all. So he said, "Okay, come up with twenty ideas." He came back in an hour and everyone had twenty ideas. Some were good and some were bad, but they'd all managed to get twenty ideas.

Don't Fall in Love

What's just as bad as being too judgemental is not being judgemental enough. You have an idea and you fall head over heels in love with it and you stop thinking.

It might be a great idea, but it's probably not. It's usually the ideas that you have after sweating over the problem for a bit, which are the best. Try not to get too fixated on one idea. Just write it down and carry on thinking.

Feed the Mind

As you write down each idea, it's not just being recorded on paper; it's also being etched into your brain. And it's not just that you're memorizing that particular idea, you're also creating material for further ideas.

Einstein talked about ideas coming from "combinatory play" and Steve Jobs said, "Creativity is just connecting things." So the more thoughts you have about a problem, the more interesting the combination of ideas you can have.

The writer James Altucher came up with the concept of increasing your idea muscle by coming up with ten ideas a day. Each day he picks a different subject. It could be anything "Ten businesses I can start", "Ten ways to give me more free time", "Ten ways to make my daily commute more interesting". The important thing is to force yourself to come up with ten. As he says, the first three will be fairly easy, but the last few can be like squeezing blood out of a stone.

I think it's a great idea and would thoroughly recommend it. Again with this exercise, it's not about the quality, it's about the quantity. But by freeing yourself from the pressure of having to have good ideas, you will find that by having lots of ideas you will naturally start having interesting ideas.

> ## 66 By having lots of ideas you will naturally start having interesting ideas. 99

What's really important are those last few ideas. Whether they're good ideas or not, it's the effort you put in on these that will give you a more creative mind. As in the gym, it's the last set of reps that you struggle with, rather than the first set, which is most beneficial. In the words of the late, great Maya Angelou, "You can't use up creativity. The more you use, the more you have."

32 Think Like a Child

"Every child is an artist. The problem is how to remain an artist once we grow up."
Pablo Picasso

We're always being told if we want to be creative we need to think like a child. Well now there's scientific proof to back it up.

In a study conducted at the North Dakota State University, they discovered that the secret of finding your inner child is not as previously thought – snips and snails and puppy dog tails for men or sugar and spice and all things nice for women. It's imagining yourself as a child.

For the study they took a group of college students and split them into two groups. They asked the first group to write a short essay: "Imagine school is cancelled for today. What would you do, think, and feel?" The second group were asked to write a similar essay, but with one difference to the question: "Imagine you are seven years old and school is cancelled for today. What would you do, think, and feel?"

After approximately five minutes of writing, each participant was asked to complete a version of the Torrance Test of Creative Thinking. What they found was the students who had imagined they were seven years old, showed significantly higher levels of originality in their thoughts.

Simply by imagining yourself as a free-thinking imaginative seven-year-old, it can make you more creative.

To be really open in our thinking, we need to be restricted.

To be really open in our thinking, we need to be restricted.

In the North Dakota University study, they weren't just asked to imagine they were a child; they were asked to imagine they were "a seven-year-old". Being that specific helps focus the mind and helps you break away from any unconscious blocks in your thinking.

What was also interesting about the study was that the people who seemed to show the most improvement in creative ability were the most introverted ones. The ones most worried about being judged and being wrong.

By thinking like a seven-year-old you're given the right to be wrong. Without this straitjacket of having to come up with the "right" or the "best" answer, we are free to let our imaginations run wild.

The trouble is from school onwards there's so much pressure to be "right". Sir Ken Robinson, whose TED talk "Do Schools Kill Creativity?"[1] is the most watched TED talk with over 34 million views, believes many schools kill creativity for penalizing children for being wrong. He says, "If you're not prepared to be wrong, you'll never come up with anything original."

And now with social media playing such a central role in so many people's lives, the pressure to conform is even greater. What's cool and what's not cool is just another way of saying what's right and what's wrong.

Nowadays both children and adults are not just being judged by their small group of friends and family, but by the whole world.

And this pressure to conform, whether conscious or unconscious, is having a big effect on how creative we are.

Every year thousands of people worldwide take the Torrence creativity test as well as an IQ test. And for every generation the scores usually go up by about 10 points. This rise in ability in both intellectual and creative tests is linked to a phenomenon called the Flynn effect.

You can hear more about this in James Flynn's TED talk: "Why our IQ levels are higher than our grandparents"[2], but basically, taking America as an example, in 1900, only 3% of people practised professions that were deemed "cognitively demanding". Today, 35% of us do, and we have all learned to be more flexible in the way that we think about problems.

So IQ and creativity scores kept rising as predicted until 1990. In 1990 while IQ scores continued to rise, Torrence creativity test scores started to drop.

Kyung Hee Kim from William & Mary College in Virginia analysed almost 300,000 Torrance scores of children and adults. Since 1990 he noticed creativity scores have consistently inched downward. "It's very clear, and the decrease is very significant," he said. This decrease in score is particularly noticeable in school age children.

I think it's no coincidence that the peer group pressure machine, or "the Internet" as it is commonly known, really gained public awareness in the 90s. By the mid to late 90s the Internet was growing by 100% a year.

But ironically, while we're becoming less creative, creativity is seen as more and more important. Look at this 2010 IBM study of 1,500 chief executive officers from 60 countries and 33 industries worldwide. What did they see as the most important leadership quality – creativity.[3]

Most important leadership qualities over the next five years

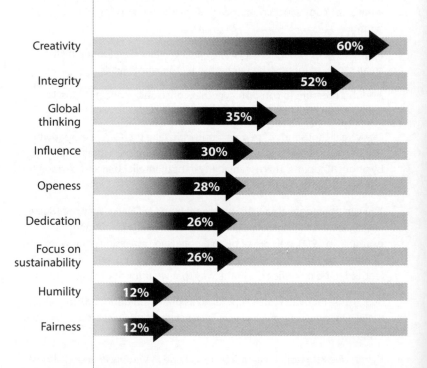

Quality	Percentage
Creativity	60%
Integrity	52%
Global thinking	35%
Influence	30%
Openess	28%
Dedication	26%
Focus on sustainability	26%
Humility	12%
Fairness	12%

And you can tell this is a real survey by hard-nosed business leaders. Humility and fairness are last on 12%.

So while we are valuing creativity more and more, it's becoming harder to escape from our fear of being wrong.

And that's why the "think like a seven-year-old" exercise is so useful. It's generally believed that peer group pressure comes in around the age of nine, so by thinking like a seven-year-old, you're going back to that time when you weren't judged, when you could be wrong and no one thought any worse of you for it.

So the next time you're getting a group of people together to solve a problem, why not put a big bowl of sweets in the middle of the table (the best way to channel your inner seven-year-old) and ask everyone to write down their ideas on how as a seven-year-old they would solve the problem. Even if a solution doesn't come out of it, it will certainly get everyone in a more creative frame of mind.

66 While we are valuing creativity more and more, it's becoming harder to escape from our fear of being wrong. 99

Of course you wouldn't want real seven-year-olds trying to solve your problem. It would be chaos. You want an adult, with all their experience, channeling the open and curious nature of a seven-year-old.

As Charles Baudelaire wrote in *The Painter of Modern Life*, "Genius is no more than childhood recaptured at will, childhood equipped now with man's physical means to express itself, and with the analytical mind that enables it to bring order into the sum of experience, involuntarily amassed."

If you can really get a roomful of adults to think like seven-year-olds, you'll have a group of people who aren't worried who had what idea, or what the boss thinks. And most importantly you'll have a roomful of people who want to be creators and not critics.

33 Don't Finish

"When you are going good, stop writing."
Ernest Hemingway

When it comes to writing or creating anything, people always talk about the fear of the blank sheet of paper.

But it's not really a fear of paper, unless you've got Papyrophobia and then it is.

It's the fear of a blank mind.

But there's an easy way to hack your way out of having a blank mind. When you sit down to work on a project, don't finish.

Say, for example, you're writing a long work document, the natural inclination would be to stop where you find a natural ending: at the end of a thought or, at the very least, the end of a paragraph.

You're dotting the i's and crossing the t's and leaving it neat and tidy for tomorrow. But the trouble is, putting your project to bed like this also puts your mind to sleep and that's the last thing you want.

The project might only be half way through, but to your mind it's done and dusted. The next day when you come back to it, you really are starting afresh.

> **When you sit down to work on a project, don't finish.**

You need to re-engage your mind in the project and this can be hard. You can't really grasp that thought that seemed so clear the night before. And then because it's not coming easily, you start to feel blocked and negative emotions start arising about your own ability. You get distracted by emails and then when you come back to it later, getting into it again seems an even more daunting task.

Writer's Hack

Well, Ernest Hemingway had an answer to this problem. When he stopped writing he didn't leave it at a natural neat ending point of a chapter or even a paragraph. He wanted to leave his writing with a sharp jagged edge so it couldn't be ignored. So he would always stop mid sentence.

This is what he said about the practice: "You write until you come to a place where you still have your juice and know what will happen next and you stop and try to live through until the next day when you hit it again."

Firstly and most obviously, by stopping when you know what you want to write next, makes it a lot easier to start again the next day.

But more importantly, you're engaging your brain and tying it to the project. The brain doesn't like unfinished business, so by stopping mid-sentence you're keeping it involved. That's what Hemingway meant when he said, "you stop and try to live through until the next day when you hit it again." Your mind is actually desperate to get back to working on it.

And what's even better is when you switch off, your unconscious won't. It'll keep thinking about it, so when you sit down to write, not only will you know what to write, but new ideas might start bubbling up from your unconscious as well.

Of course, the hard thing is to stop writing when it's going well. You want to make the most of this purple patch. But you have to be tough on yourself. Pick a time or a number of words and after that, stop.

Hemingway passed on his writing hack to another great writer, Roald Dahl, who said this about it: "Make yourself stop, put your pencil down and you walk away. And you can't wait to get back because you know what you want to say next and that's lovely and you have to try and do that. ... If you stop when you are stuck, then you are in trouble!"

It's simple really.

When you are going good, stop wri

34 Take Part in Name Calling

"The beginning of wisdom is to call things by their own names."
Chinese Proverb

"You need to get in touch with your emotions" is a phrase you hear a lot these days, in relation to growing as a person.

But do you need to get in touch with them?

There are lots of emotions I don't want to get in touch with: intimidated, scared, insecure, lonely, unhappy, angry, upset, sad, patronized, humiliated … I could go on about the appointment with my doctor, but I won't.

The fact is there are a lot of emotions that can have quite an overpowering effect on us. But our emotions are there to help us. We need our feelings to signal to us about the dangers and opportunities that we face from within and without. But when our emotions get too strong they just take over and we can't function properly.

But there is a simple technique that can really help to diffuse negative emotions. Name them. I don't mean give each emotion its own pet name: "This is my insecurity, but I call it 'Norman'". No, what I mean is when you feel an overpowering emotion, just say the name of it.

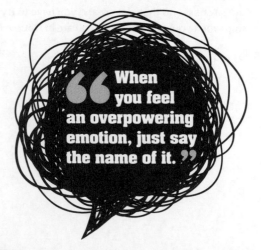

When you feel an overpowering emotion, just say the name of it.

Obviously if you're in the company of someone you say it in your head, but if you're alone, saying it out loud can give it more authority.

For instance if someone says they don't like what you're wearing, you might say "humiliated", or if some one cuts you up when you're driving, you might say "angry".

> **Attaching a word to our messy emotions is a very effective way to lessen their impact.**

Now this isn't just some new age mumbo jumbo; there is some real science behind it. Recently, researchers discovered that attaching a word to our messy emotions is a very effective way to lessen their impact. In a series of studies by UCLA psychologist Matthew D. Lieberman, participants who attached labels to emotions like "anger" or "fear" had less activity in the amygdala, the part of the brain that governs our fight-or-flight response. But these individuals also had more activity in the right ventrolateral prefrontal cortex, or the thinking part of the brain.

Labelling their feelings shifted them from an emotional state to a thinking state. Suddenly your mind is changing its focus from the emotion "anger" to the word "anger".

Lieberman explained: "In the same way you hit the brake when you're driving when you see a yellow light, when you put feelings into words, you seem to be hitting the brakes on your emotional responses."

Another study on whether naming can help reduce negative emotions was run at UCLA by Dr Katerina Kircanski and her colleagues.

They wanted to discover whether people's use of language could help treat phobias and irrational fears of things. For their test, they used a fear of spiders.

They divided the 88 participants into three groups. The first group had to verbally label their negative emotion (affect labelling). The second group had to substitute neutral phrases about their negative experience (reappraisal), and the third to make up a sentence about an unrelated familiar object (distraction).

They measured the results in two ways. The first was skin conductance (the skin momentarily becomes a better conductor of electricity when either external or internal stimuli occur that are physiologically arousing). The second measure was simply for the participants to self-report their fear on a scale of zero to a hundred from "no fear" to "extreme fear".

When it came to personally reporting how the participants felt there was very little difference in the three groups. But in the physiological test, the group that verbalized their fear showed the greatest reduction in skin conductance response. Dr Kircanski said it might be because individuals don't expect to feel less fear from labelling a negative emotion.

Of course your feelings won't disappear, and you don't want them to. They play an important role in helping us understand and cope with people, situations and experiences. But just naming the feeling can help soothe negative emotions and stop us responding impulsively, drowning in negative feelings, or becoming aggressive in a counter-productive way.

> **Just naming the feeling can help soothe negative emotions.**

You and I

I'd just been writing this in my office at home in the evening. I'd gone out to have some dinner and when I came back into the office, I switched on the light and saw a big spider on the wall. I didn't say "scared" under my breath as I'm not scared of spiders. But it was very strange. I expected to turn round and see a researcher in a white coat, standing in the corner of the room with a clipboard.

But if I was scared of spiders, I would be better off saying to myself "You shouldn't let it get to you" rather than "I won't let it get to me."

This is the next finding in my "talking-to-yourself" research.

When you give yourself motivational speeches in your head (and 96% of adults do), it will lead to better performance if you use "you" rather than "I". So instead of saying to yourself "I can do it", you should say "You can do it."

Sanda Dolcos at the University of Illinois at Urbana–Champaign and Dolores Albarracin at the University of Pennsylvania conducted a series of experiments on the subject.

66 When you give yourself motivational speeches in your head, it will lead to better performance if you use 'you' rather than 'I'. 99

In the first experiment, they had 95 undergraduates imagine they were a character in a sketch, and that character was facing a choice. They were asked to write down the advice they would give themselves in making this choice, and half were told to use "I" in their instructions while the other half were told to use "you."

Afterward, the participants were asked to complete anagrams. Those who had used "you" in their advice to their character completed more anagrams than those who had used "I".

They also ran a test where they asked 135 psychology students to write down advice to themselves about exercising for the next two weeks. The ones using "you" in their advice planned to do more exercise during those two weeks and also reported more positive attitudes toward it than the students giving themselves first-person advice.

In another study, conducted by University of Michigan's Ethan Kross, participants were told they had to give a speech to a panel of judges on why they were qualified for their dream job. And they had to give it in five minutes without notes.

In the study they found that those who worked through their stress about giving a speech using "you" rather than "I" performed better and were less bothered by anxieties. When people use the second-person pronoun "it allows them to give themselves objective, helpful feedback", said Ethan Kross.

So what's behind the "you" effect? The researchers speculated that second-person self-talk may have this beneficial effect because it cues memories of receiving support and encouragement from others, especially in childhood.

I think when you say "I", it's more of a challenge to yourself, whereas when you say "you", it's much more supportive and much more likely to instill confidence.

Time to Talk It Out

Have you ever found yourself walking down the aisles in a supermarket, looking for a particular item and then muttering the name of the product at the same time? Well, whatever the other shoppers thought of you, you were actually using a very helpful cognitive tool.

Past research has shown that self-directed speech can help guide behaviours for children, such as tying shoelaces or other step-by-step tasks. But Gary Lupyan and Daniel Swingley from the University of Wisconsin have found the same can be true for adults.

As long as you know what an object looks like, if you say its name out loud, you can speed up the process of finding it.

In one experiment, volunteers were shown 20 pictures of various objects and asked to look for a specific one, such as a banana. In half of the trials, participants were asked to repeatedly say what they were looking for out loud to themselves; in the others, they were asked to remain silent.

The researchers found self-directed speech helped people find objects more quickly by about a tenth of a second, which might not sound like much, but it is when you see it as a percentage of the average time it took participants to find an item, which was 1.2 to 2 seconds.

"The general take-home point is that language is not just a system of communication, but I'm arguing it can augment perception, augment thinking," Lupyan told *Livescience*.

The benefits lie much further than finding fruit in the supermarket or cheese in your fridge. Speaking helps any search, particularly when there is a strong association between the name and the look of an object. If you're organizing elements for a project or presentation, or looking for documents on your computer, try naming the items out loud and it should help speed up the process and use up less mental energy.

35 Stay Focused

> "You will never reach your destination if you stop and throw stones at every dog that barks."
> *Winston Churchill*

Staying focused is something that's harder and harder in this age of information. Did you know that 90% of all the data in the world has been created over the last two years?

The lure of social media is constantly dragging us away from important tasks. You think you'll just have a quick look and before you know it, half an hour has passed. The distraction of email is just as bad, but we console ourselves that "it's work".

While there's more and more information vying for our attention, our ability to focus is, if anything, getting worse.

It's not helped by information being fed to us in smaller and smaller chunks. Look at movie trailers for example. In the 1950s, the average amount of cuts per minute was twelve – now the average is thirty-eight; over three times as much.

> **The lure of social media is constantly dragging us away from important tasks.**

But the trouble isn't just the speed and the amount of information that's thrown at us, it's that our brains can't multi-task.

David Meyer, director of the Brain, Cognition and Action Laboratory at Michigan University and one of the country's leading experts on multi-tasking, says "You can't do two cognitively complicated tasks at once. When you're on the phone and writing an email at the same time, you're actually switching back and forth between them, since there's only one mental and neural channel through which language flows."

It's been known for some time that when our brains are focused on a task, we can fail to see other things that are in plain sight. This phenomenon is known as "inattentional blindness". One of the famous examples of this is the "invisible gorilla" experiment (www.theinvisiblegorilla.com/videos.html).

Viewers are asked to watch a video of players passing around a basketball and count the number of passes. Whilst focused on counting, they end up failing to observe a man in a gorilla suit walking across the centre of the screen.

But more worrying, new results show that our visual field does not need to be cluttered with other objects to cause this "blindness". Focusing on remembering something we have only just seen is enough to make us unaware of things that happen around us.

Professor Nilli Lavie from UCL Institute of Cognitive Neuroscience, said:

"An example of where this is relevant in the real world is when people are following directions on a sat nav while driving. Our research would suggest that focusing on remembering the directions we've just seen on the screen means that we're more likely to fail to observe other hazards around us on the road, for example an approaching motorbike or a pedestrian on a crossing, even though we may be 'looking' at where we're going."

It's as if the visual pathway to the brain is a single-track path with information having to take turns to travel along it. Basically it means that even though the eyes "see" the object, the brain may not.

Unfortunately, the only way to solve the sat nav problem is not to use one; but there are other ways to improve our focus.

Single-Tasking

Firstly, rather than spending an hour "multi-tasking", split your time up. So instead of writing a document, making phone calls and checking emails all at the same time, spent twenty minutes on each. Twenty minutes on the document, twenty minutes on phone calls and twenty minutes on emails. If you can manage it, you'll find you write better and have more insightful conversations and just as importantly, your mind will stay fresher.

Focus Training

Having a lack of focus is very much like having a lack of fitness. As with physical exercise, you build up your stamina over time. The same can be done with your focus.

Try performing a task, without letting yourself get distracted for thirty minutes. It can be any task but it's important that it's not an activity you love, so you have to make some effort to stay focused. Then for three or four days, increase the period by five or ten minutes each day.

You don't need to push beyond an hour. But just by spending three or four days building up your concentration, you'll really notice the difference.

The important thing is not to take a break in that time, not even for a minute.

A Busy Mind Is a Focused Mind

What Nilli Lavie found helped keep people focused, was making the task more visually demanding. That meant adding more colours and shapes. So if you are focusing on learning something, use different coloured pens and different symbols for indexing the information. This takes up more of your brain's processing power and doesn't leave it with any inclination or energy to wander.

Don't Waste the Power Hour

Of course there's no point in trying to be really focused at the end of a long day, it's just not going to happen. We are at our most alert first thing in the morning, so don't waste that first hour looking through emails. Give yourself one hour focused thinking on your current task and after that look at emails/check social media.

But make sure you stick to one hour. Your brain will find it a lot easier to stay focused when it knows it can bunk off after exactly an hour and look through emails and social media updates.

The trouble is, distraction feels good. Your brain's reward circuit lights up when you multi-task (even though you're not actually multi-tasking, just getting distracted a lot) which means that you get an emotional high when you're doing a lot at once. So as long as it knows it's going to get its reward after an hour, it will be happy.

David Rock, co-founder of the NeuroLeadership Institute says: "A distraction is an alert; it says to your brain, 'Orient your attention here now; this could be dangerous.' Your brain's reaction is automatic and virtually unstoppable."

The secret is not to get distracted. So for that one hour, make sure the only connection is between you and your project; switch everything else off.

66 The secret is not to get distracted. 99

Rock studied thousands of people and found that we are only truly focused for an average of only six hours per week.

So try to give yourself one fully focused hour every weekday morning. Use it to work on an important project without any distraction.

It's not the best way to focus; it's the only way to focus.

36 Work Messy

"If a cluttered desk is a sign of a cluttered mind, of what, then, is an empty desk a sign?"

Albert Einstein

You walk into an Apple store and it's uncluttered and beautifully laid out. In the same way Apple products are about clean lines and simple design. So it would be fairly safe to assume Steve Jobs' desk would have been a perfect example of Zen minimalism.

Wrong, it was a complete tip.

Other famous exemplars of the messy desk are Einstein, Mark Twain, Alexander Fleming, Mark Zuckerberg and Alan Turing.

All in very different fields, but all very creative thinkers.

The question is, were their desks messy because they were creative, or were they creative because they had messy desks?

Was the real reason that one of Fleming's Petri dishes got mould all over it and so helped him invent penicillin, because it got lost under a pile of junk on his desk?

Unlikely. And of course there's more to being creative than just having a messy desk. But research lead by Kathleen Vohs,[1] a professor at the University of Minnesota, has found that you do actually get a creativity boost when you work in a messy space.

> **You do actually get a creativity boost when you work in a messy space.**

In their first study they created two rooms: a tidy one with books and papers neatly stacked, and a messy one with papers and books strewn all over the place.

They then got over 180 adults to attend what they said was a consumer choice study. Each individual was assigned either the tidy or the messy room. They then asked the participants if they'd like a fruit smoothie from the deli.

They created two versions of the menu. Half of the subjects saw a menu that had the word "classic" highlighting the health boost option, whereas the other half saw the health boost highlighted by the word "new".

When the subjects were in the tidy room they chose the "classic" drink almost twice as often. When the subjects were in the messy room, they chose the "new" drink more than twice as often.

Therefore, people greatly preferred convention in the tidy room and novelty in the messy room.

The next test wasn't just to see if people were more inclined to newness, but to see if messiness actually encouraged creativity.

They assigned a group of individuals messy or neat rooms as before. But this time they asked them to think of new uses for ping-pong balls.

The participants from both rooms wrote down about the same numbers of solutions. But when the solutions were analysed by independent judges, it was found that the ideas that came from people in the messy room were seen as 28% more creative.

Amazingly, almost five times as many of the ideas that were judged as "highly creative", like cutting open the balls and using them as ice cube trays, or attaching them to chair legs to protect floors, came from people in the messy room.

Researchers at Northwestern University found the same results when they tried their own messy/tidy room experiment. They found that subjects in a messy room drew more creative pictures and were quicker to solve a challenging brainteaser puzzle than subjects in a tidy room.

Our brains are very impressionable, so the unconscious cues of disorder in the messy room make us think "messy". This disorderly thinking is an ideal state to be in when trying to come up with innovative and unexpected ideas.

Maybe it's an argument for moving away from the current trend of minimal open plan offices.

They say the basics of good interior design are space, flow and function. Well, if you want the ideas to flow, people will function better with their own space and a little bit of good old-fashioned clutter.

PART 5

Breaking Through and Innovating

The moment of insight and how to turn ideas into innovations

37 Enjoy Being Blocked

"Writing is like driving a car at night. You can see only as far as your headlights, but you can make the whole trip that way."

E.L. Doctorow

I'm sitting at my computer trying to write about creative block but I don't know how to start. This isn't the first line I've written; I've started and deleted a few already. I've got background material about being blocked and I've got various ideas of my own that I want to write about, but it's still hard getting started.

There you go, I've started. That's one of the most important things (as mentioned previously in Brainhack 20) is just to start. One of the fears people have is that what they create won't be good. People have said to me that they can't write. But of course they can write – what they really mean is they feel they can't write well.

The important thing is just to get started and not worry too much about what you're going to write or whether it's going to be any good. You're probably going to have to do some more work on it anyway.

Malcolm Gladwell says, "The solution is never to sit down and imagine that you will achieve something magical and magnificent. I write a little bit, almost every day, and if it results in two or three or (on a good day) four good paragraphs, I consider myself a lucky man. Never try to be the hare. All hail the tortoise."

> **The important thing is just to get started and not worry too much.**

Whatever field you're in, you just need to get started and don't let self-doubt get a foothold in your mind. The artist Chuck Close said this: "Inspiration is for amateurs. The rest of us just show up and get to work." And Tchaikovsky said "A self-respecting artist must not fold his hands on the pretext that he is not in the mood."

Creating anything is hard, but just because it's a struggle, it doesn't mean you're blocked.

❝ Just because it's a struggle, it doesn't mean you're blocked. ❞

It's easy to read something well written and be intimidated, thinking you could never write something like it. But just because something is effortless to read, it doesn't mean it was effortless to write. Hemingway rewrote the last page of *A Farewell to Arms* thirty-nine times before he was happy with it. He confided to F. Scott Fitzgerald in 1934, "I write one page of masterpiece to ninety-one pages of shit. I try to put the shit in the wastebasket."

One of the ways to fight the feeling of being blocked is to think about what you've achieved previously. Say you make a commitment to yourself to write a weekly blog. Once you've written one and it was okay, you will be able to do another one. The trouble is all this self-doubt starts to come in before you even start to write the second one. You begin to think you won't know what to write about.

But rather than think about it, give yourself an hour and sit down and try to work out what you can write about. Write any ideas down even if they seem rubbish. If you do get stuck, read. Read books, magazines or online articles. You're not trying to steal ideas; you're looking for a fire starter.

The most important thing is to stick at the task for an hour. Even if at the end of the hour you feel like you've got nothing, that hour will have been invaluable; you will have fed your unconscious and ideas will come later on.

Blocked Not Block

One of the worst and most damaging things is calling it writer's, or creative, block. If it is a "block" it makes it a thing; it gives it power. Really, it is about feeling blocked and it is something you need to work through.

Also, by calling your mental struggle creative block, it lets you off the hook. It's not about you: it's about the block. It's something that stands in your way like a huge wall. But it's not. It's not a thing and it's not a condition, it's all in your mind and you just have to work through it.

A Walk Round the Block

Feeling blocked can feel very different depending at what stage you are in your project.

At the start

At the start it's about looking for an idea. It's always better to sit down with an idea, and then you don't have to fear the blank sheet of paper and can get started straight away. If you follow Brainhack 25 "Take Notes", then you should always have a good list of ideas to work on. It also helps if your ideas have been maturing in your head for a little while. It's much easier when the ideas are fighting to get out rather than you having to go in search for them.

The filmmaker Werner Herzog says, "The problem isn't coming up with ideas, it is how to contain the invasion. My ideas are like uninvited guests. They don't knock on the door; they climb in through the windows like burglars who show up in the middle of the night and make a racket in the kitchen as they raid the fridge. I don't sit and ponder which one I should deal with first. The one to be wrestled to the floor before all others is the one coming at me with the most vehemence."[1]

Once you've got an idea you need to just dive into getting it down on paper and don't worry about the quality of the writing. If you start writing straight away you'll engage the mind much quicker and it'll get easier and easier as the minutes pass.

The trouble is, if you spend too much time just sitting there staring at the blank piece of paper/screen, your mind will get restless and procrastination will take over. You've got emails to read, pencils to sharpen. If you let your mind distract you from writing, it'll just be harder the next time you try to start writing again.

In the middle

You've got to the middle of whatever project you're doing and you don't know where to go. It's like walking through a forest and suddenly finding yourself back where you were five minutes ago. It can be very dispiriting. The thing is you should be proud of how far you have managed to come.

You will find an answer – you just need to keep thinking and not get too stressed. You need to think about the problem for a while, but then take a break and keep it on the back burner. If your unconscious can see that your conscious mind is really desperate for a solution, it'll put its full processing power behind solving it.

The thing with being blocked is it's all mental. If you fear it, you give it power. You'll feel totally lost and dispirited. Have faith and keep gently persevering and embrace being blocked. Because when your unconscious offers up a solution, it will have been worth waiting for.

When I've been writing these chapters, I'll often move on to a new one before I've finished a previous one. I'll then come back to the first one a day later and it's suddenly a lot clearer what I need to do to finish it.

The main thing to remember is: feeling blocked is all in the mind. If you're about to start something, just dive in and don't give your thoughts room to start to play mind games with you. If you're in the middle and feeling blocked, don't get stressed. Just keep thinking about the problem and your unconscious will eventually come to your rescue.

❝ Feeling blocked is all in the mind. ❞

38 Think Like Goldilocks

"Creativity comes from conscious facts planted in the unconscious and allowed to germinate."
Bertrand Russell

As I've mentioned in previous chapters, the unconscious mind plays a very important role in coming up with ideas. But you need to create the right conditions for this to happen. And this brainhack is all about how you create those conditions. There's no guarantee ideas will pop up from your unconscious, but it's like planting a seed; if you plant it in a sunny spot in good soil and give it plenty of water, you've given it the best chance to grow.

One of the most common misconceptions is that "creative" people have these "light bulb moments" that just pop into their heads as if from nowhere. But no one has great ideas without thinking about a problem for a long time. It only seems to come out of nowhere because it comes from your unconscious. They never just appear without a lot of hard work.

John Lennon spent five hours trying to write a song "that was meaningful and good". Finally he gave up and lay down. "Then *Nowhere Man* came, words and music, the whole damn thing, as I lay down…So letting it go is what the whole game is."

> ❝ **No one has great ideas without thinking about a problem for a long time.** ❞

If you work hard on a problem and are passionate about finding a solution, your unconscious mind will then deem it worthy of putting its processing power behind it. But one of the side effects of working hard on something is that you're likely to get to a place where you feel you can't think of any more ideas. This is often when people feel either blocked or start to feel self-doubt.

But this is when you need to follow "Goldilocks" thinking – neither too hard nor too soft. If your unconscious is to be allowed to do its stuff, you want to avoid the two extremes: on the one hand getting too stressed and on the other hand totally zoning out and doing something mindless, such as watching TV or checking up on Facebook.

You just need to keep the problem simmering away on the back burner. As John Cleese said, "This is the extraordinary thing about creativity: if you keep your mind resting against the subject in a friendly way, sooner or later you will get a reward from your unconscious."

It often helps to stop thinking about the problem altogether as Hilary Mantel said in her "Ten Rules for Writing Fiction" in *The Guardian*: "If you get stuck, get away from your desk. Take a walk, take a bath, go to sleep, make a pie, draw, listen to music, meditate, exercise; whatever you do, don't just stick there scowling at the problem. But don't make telephone calls or go to a party; if you do, other people's words will pour in where your lost words should be. Open a gap for them, create a space."

When the breakthrough or insight you've been looking for does come, it's accompanied by a surge of energy. This isn't just mental, it's actually physical.

When J.K. Rowling described getting the idea for her first book for adults she said, "I had a totally physical response you get to an idea that you know will work. It's a rush of adrenaline; it's chemical. I had it with Harry Potter and I had it with this."

> ❝ **When the breakthrough or insight you've been looking for does come, it's accompanied by a surge of energy. This isn't just mental, it's actually physical.** ❞

Scientists have found that the moment of creative insight is actually accompanied by a spike in brainwaves called gamma waves, the highest electrical frequency generated by the brain.

But what's just as interesting, is what happens before the moment of insight. There is a surge of alpha waves at the back of the head. Now alpha waves are associated with closing areas of the brain down and the back of the brain mainly deals with visual processing. At least half the brain's power is normally devoted directly or indirectly to vision.

As well as the part of the brain involved in visual processing closing down, there is a distinct change in the frontal lobes, which are the main areas of consciousness in the brain. They were almost going into sleep mode, which neuropsychologist, Rex Jung, calls "transient hypofrontality".

Your brain wants to concentrate fully on the moment of insight, so it reduces both the amount of visual information that is processed and how much conscious thinking goes on. It's as if at that moment you go into a sort of "creative trance".

It's why if you ever see someone at the point when they have an idea, they look down or stare into space or if they're on a walk, they'll suddenly stop when the idea occurs to them.

Of course if you haven't experienced one of these "light bulb moments", this may all seem a bit alien to you. But are you sure you haven't?

Have you ever been doing a crossword puzzle and found yourself stuck on a particular crossword clue? You keep thinking about it, but it just won't come. Finally, you give up. You stop thinking about it and move on to another clue, or go to make a cup of tea. Then suddenly, as if from nowhere, the answer to the clue you were stuck on just pops into your head.

When Archimedes had his famous moment of insight, he jumped out of his bath and ran naked through the streets of Syracuse, shouting "Eureka". He hadn't just got the answer to seven across, but it's the same mental process that was at work.

Whether it's just the answer to a crossword clue or something bigger, the experience of an idea coming out of nowhere still comes as a real surprise. Paul Simon described the moment *Bridge Over Troubled Water* came to him: "One minute it wasn't there and the next minute the whole line was there. It was one of the shocking moments in my songwriting career."

It's no surprise then, that in Ancient Greece they didn't actually believe individuals were creative. The Greeks believed that the muses were real. To them, they were goddesses who were considered the source of all knowledge, which were then invoked by the writer or artist.

And take the word "genius". It actually comes from Ancient Rome and doesn't refer to a gifted individual, but a guiding spirit. The achievements of exceptional people were seen as an indication of the presence of a particularly powerful "genius". In fact, it was only during the Renaissance in the 14th century that creativity was first seen as the ability of a gifted "individual".

39 Take a Walk, Have a Shower

"Thoughts come clearly while one walks."
Thomas Mann

It's almost become a cliché: "I get my best ideas in the shower", but like all clichés it's based in truth.

It's not just showers; it's any simple mundane activity that doesn't require much thought: walking, cycling, mowing the lawn. Agatha Christie said, "The best time for planning a book is while you're doing the dishes."

I will go into more detail on why these activities are so good for coming up with ideas later, but first I have to reiterate what I've said in the last two chapters: good ideas don't appear out of nowhere; you need to have thought long and hard about a question beforehand. You have to be passionate about finding a solution and a little obsessed.

If you've done this, then that's when these simple physical activities can help you. The door between the conscious and unconscious only opens one way. You can't go into your unconscious, but ideas can come out. What these activities do is oil the hinges of the door to your unconscious, to help it open more easily.

❝ You have to be passionate about finding a solution and a little obsessed. ❞

Professor Jonathan Schooler of the University of California created an experiment to test out this theory. He took three groups of people and gave them each a minute to think of as many unusual uses for a house brick as they could.

They were all then given a two-minute break. While they rested, the first group was told to just sit there and think of nothing. The second had the simple and unchallenging task of sorting Lego bricks by colour and the third had to build a house out of Lego. After that, they were all given another minute to think of some more uses for a house brick.

The group that did the worst were the ones who had been concentrating and focused on building a house out of Lego. And the group that did the best were the ones whose minds were mildly stimulated and just had to sort the Lego by colour.

Now you might think that the ones who had nothing to think about should do best. But as soon as they'd finished the initial task their minds were thinking conscious thoughts about their life, what they were going to do later, what they were going to eat. Whereas the group who had the mundane task of sorting the Lego bricks into different colours, had that to occupy their conscious minds, leaving their unconscious to carry on thinking about uses for a household brick.

All the mundane activities that I mentioned at the start still require some conscious thought, but you can almost do them on autopilot. And as soon as the brain sees the chance to go onto autopilot, it takes it. It sees it as a chance to relax.

When you're focusing on a task, the "cognitive control network" is running the show. At the heart of this network is the prefrontal cortex, the brain's command centre for decisions, goals and behaviours. Now the cognitive control network (the active network) uses up a lot of energy, so when the brain sees the opportunity to rest, it will.

So when you're doing a task almost on autopilot, it will switch to what is called the "default mode network" (the resting network). It's the equivalent of you flopping down in a comfy chair at the end of the day.

Incredibly the brain will use any opportunity to switch to the resting network. A study by Tamami Nakano of Osaka University revealed that the brain switches briefly to the resting network even for the very brief period when we blink.

But what it shows, is when the brain's got the chance to switch from the active network to the resting network, it will. And while the resting network is in control, the conscious mind is having a breather and the mind is allowed to wander. At this time the door to the unconscious may not be fully opened, but it is at least ajar.

The Cat's Away, the Mice Will Play

The reason I think this is such a productive area for ideas is because it creates a new type of thought; you're not consciously thinking, but at the same time you're not daydreaming. I would call it "dreamthinking".

Take the Agatha Christie quote where she says she finds the best time for plotting a book is when she's doing the dishes. If she was just thinking focused conscious thoughts, she would have no access to the more surprising and more lateral thoughts that come with daydreaming and the unconscious. But at the same time if the mind went off on a daydream it would just wander through various thoughts and wouldn't be able to concentrate on the plot of a book.

As Tamami Nakano's study showed, the brain can switch to the resting network for the briefest of periods. So I think when, for instance, you have a shower you're in this "dreamthinking" zone, whereby you're constantly switching from thinking to mind-wandering states. Engaging, disengaging and then engaging again.

Walk the Walk

Walking, like taking a shower, is an activity we can almost do on autopilot, so is an ideal activity for the brain to give the active network a rest and switch to the mind-wandering of the resting network.

Dr Marily Oppezzo and Daniel Schwartz from Stanford University decided to test whether it was the actual act of walking that made people more creative.

What they expected to find was that walking outside in the fresh air with inspiring scenery would be, but that walking inside on a treadmill wouldn't.

Dr Oppezzo says she thought "walking outside would blow everything out of the water, but walking on a treadmill in a small, boring room still had strong results, which surprised me."

But whether it was walking inside or outside, the participants' creative output went up by an average of 60% compared to people sitting down. It wasn't to do with the environment, it was to do with the repetitive act of walking, which switched the mind from the active network to the mind-wandering resting network.

In total, 81% of the participants saw an increase in their creativity when they were walking. Also when the participants took a second test after walking, they were still more creative, showing the positive effects of walking continued even after they sat down again.

These results would come as no surprise to many famous creative people throughout history who swore by the value of walking. Nietzsche said, "All truly great thoughts are conceived while walking." Beethoven, Tchaikovsky, Freud, Milton, Dickens, Darwin, Watt and Poincaré all valued it as a way of nurturing creativity.

Dickens would never miss his afternoon walks through London and in the countryside. Dickens said if he couldn't walk "far and fast" he would "explode and perish". He would often walk up to thirty miles a day.

Darwin created his own version of the treadmill and had a circular gravel path created in his garden, that he would walk round and round until a certain problem was solved.

James Watt came up with the idea for his steam engine while out on a Sunday afternoon walk: "I had not walked farther than the golf-house when the whole thing was arranged in my mind."

Poincaré, frustrated with his failure in solving some arithmetical questions, went to spend a few days by the seaside. "One morning, walking on the bluff, the idea came to me, with just the same characteristics of brevity, suddenness and immediate certainty."

Walk and Talk

It's just as valuable today and perhaps more so, as long as you can manage to keep your mobile in your pocket. Steve Jobs was a huge advocate of walking as a method of working on problems, but also as a way of holding meetings. Co-founder of Twitter, Jack Dorsey, and Mark Zuckerberg of Facebook are also big fans of walking meetings.

Driving can also be a good activity for accessing this mind wandering state. But obviously you need to be driving a route you know well. In fact in a survey a few years ago, Americans chose the car as the place where they did their most creative thinking.

What's important is that it's an activity that you can do without really thinking about it. One that doesn't require a great deal of concentration, so the focused thought of the prefrontal cortex can switch off.

If you want your mind to relax, you've got to get active.

66 If you want your mind to relax, you've got to get active. 99

40 Switch Off

> "Boredom is your window ... Once this window opens, don't try to shut it; on the contrary, throw it wide open."
> *Joseph Brodsky*

Most of these hacks are about actively doing something to change how your brain works. This one's about not doing something. It's an un-hack. It's about not using your mobile phone.

The average smartphone user checks their phone at least 150 times a day and 58% of smartphone users don't go an hour without checking their phones.

It's not surprising they're called smartphones, because they certainly know how to push *our* buttons. Our prefrontal cortex (the part of our brain that expresses our personality and makes decisions) has a novelty bias. Basically, it's hijacked by anything new. And smartphones are brimming with newness.

Also if you're already doing something when you grab your phone you're multitasking and thereby creating a dopamine-addiction feedback loop. We're turning our brains into drug addicts. Effectively we're rewarding it for losing focus and for constantly searching for external stimulation.

Of course there's no denying how useful smartphones can be, but the way we get them out as soon as we have an idle moment is cutting out the opportunity for our mind to wander.

Christopher Nolan, the director of *The Dark Knight* trilogy, *Inception* and *Interstellar*, doesn't have a phone. In fact, he doesn't even have an email account. He likes to be disconnected from the online world because he says it gives him time to think.

I'm not saying give up your phone. I know I couldn't. I'm just saying, don't turn to it as soon as you've got a quiet moment.

Imagine you're in a coffee shop waiting for a friend who's ten minutes late. Do you sit and stare out of the window and let your mind wander or do you grab your phone?

The urge of course is to take out your phone. It's easy to feel like staring out of the window is wasting time, whereas if we spend the time catching up on emails or social media we feel it's time well spent.

But it's important to let yourself get bored. Getting bored is good. It's when we daydream, when our minds wander and this is a very important part of coming up with new ideas.

The time when you allow yourself to daydream, is one of the times when your mind's at it's busiest. "Perceptual decoupling" is what cognitive psychologist Jonathan Smallwood calls it. He says, "In a very deep way there's a close link between originality, novelty, and creativity and these sort of spontaneous thoughts that we generate when our minds are idle."

❝❝ It's important to let yourself get bored. ❞

A recent study by Pennsylvania State University researchers Karen Gasper and Brianna Middlewood found that being bored helps promote creative association and pushes one to find deeper meaning and satisfaction.

After watching videos that were designed to create certain emotions, the participants took creativity tests. Of all the emotions elicited: relaxed, elated, bored and distressed; the ones who were bored outperformed all the others.

At the University of Central Lancashire, Sandi Mann and Rebekah Cadman ran their own boredom-related study. They took two groups, one that had to do nothing and one that had to do the mind-numbing task of copying phone numbers out of a phone book.

They followed this with an exercise to think of as many possible uses for a pair of plastic cups. The group that had suffered through the phone book task thought of more creative uses.

Sandi Mann said, "One of the by-products of boredom is it seems to make us more creative. This is because it's a connection between mind-wandering and daydreaming that allows new connections in our brain to form and come up with creative solutions."

Bored Yet?

We are so scared of being bored that we rarely spend time alone with our own thoughts. Most of the time we're either interacting with someone, busy doing something, going somewhere or reading or watching something.

> **" We are so scared of being bored that we rarely spend time alone with our own thoughts. "**

I've been involved in running a day's workshop where part of the day involves participants spending two hours on their own. They can't use phones or computers and aren't allowed to talk to any of the other participants. They can either go for a walk on their own or just sit and think.

At the end they always remark about what a powerful and sometimes quite emotional experience it is. It gave them new ideas, new directions and sometimes helped them find the missing piece to an old problem.

Not All Daydreamers Are Created Equal

What's interesting though, is you have to be aware that you are daydreaming for it to be of value creatively.

Jonathan Schooler of University of California, Santa Barbara, ran tests where participants were given a boring activity and had to press a button as soon as they noticed their mind had wandered. However, some people failed to notice their minds had wandered. They didn't press the button and only realized their mind had wandered when prodded by the researcher. According to Schooler's data, these individuals didn't exhibit any increased creativity.

So to be more creative you need to be aware that you're daydreaming. But then, as soon as you become aware that you're daydreaming, you're not daydreaming any more!

The secret is to become aware of your daydreams at the point when an interesting thought or insight arises. This isn't something we can really control. But if your conscious mind has been grappling with a problem and is passionate about finding an answer, when a new insight arises in your daydream, your conscious mind will naturally grab it.

If you're passionate about finding an answer to a problem the interplay between your conscious and unconscious will happen naturally.

So the next time you're bored and go to grab your phone, try and fight the urge. We're thinking all the time, but it's only when your mind is idle that you actually get to listen to your own thoughts.

> 66 **We're thinking all the time, but it's only when your mind is idle that you actually get to listen to your own thoughts.** 99

41 Think When You're Tired

> "There is a class of fancies, of exquisite delicacy......where the confines of the waking world blend with those of the world of dreams. I am aware of these 'fancies' only when I am upon the very brink of sleep ..."
>
> *Edgar Allan Poe*

Are you an early bird or a night owl?

Whichever you are, you probably think the most productive time would be the morning if you're an early bird or the end of the day if you're a night owl. Well, yes and no. It depends what type of work you're doing.

If it were analytical work that requires a focused brain, you'd be right. But if it's more of a creative problem and requires more lateral thinking, you're at your best when you're not at your best. If you're tired, your brain is not so good at focusing on a task or filtering out distractions. Your mind will wander more and therefore you'll be far more likely to create new connections and come up with unexpected ideas.

Professor Mareike Wieth from Albion College, Michigan, discovered this in a study looking at the optimal time for creativity. She said, "People intuitively know there are certain times of the day when they are better at certain tasks, but I've always wanted to test that."

So with her colleague Rose Zacks, they got 428 students to fill in a questionnaire to find out whether they were "morning people" or "evening people". It's a standard psychological questionnaire featuring questions such as, "Approximately what time would you get up if you were entirely free to plan your day?" and "How much do you depend upon an alarm clock?" The questionnaire was developed in 1976 by researchers to measure your circadian rhythm (biological clock). It's called the ... wait for it – "morningness-eveningness questionnaire" (that's its real name, but then after all, it was thought up in the 70s). But it is a serious questionnaire, which you can try out for yourself: www.chem.unt.edu/~./djtaylor/extra/meq.pdf.

Based on those answers, participants were categorized on a five-point scale ranging from an extreme morning lark to neutral to an extreme night owl. They were then randomly assigned to an 8:30 a.m. or 4 p.m. testing session. During the session, students were given four minutes apiece to solve six problems. Half were "analytic problems", which could be figured out "by working incrementally toward the solution". The others were "insight problems". Solving these generally entailed reaching a dead end before going back and reconsidering initial assumptions.

The results showed that being a bit sleepy was definitely beneficial to creative thought. While performance on the analytic problems was largely unaffected by the clock, when people were tested during their "least optimal time of day", they were significantly more effective at solving insight puzzles. (On one problem, their performance increased by nearly 50%.)

❝ Being a bit sleepy is definitely beneficial to creative thought. ❞

It's not reported if all the night owl students actually managed to make it to the lab by 8.30 a.m., however.

Tired Ideas

This idea of being most creative when we're tired is taken a step further where people try to tap into the state between wakefulness and sleep. This transitional state between sleeping and waking up is called the hypnopompic state. The hypnagogic state is the experience of the transitional state from being awake to going to sleep.

Two of the most famous proponents of this were Salvador Dali and Thomas Edison. Not the most expected of bedfellows, but in their own fields they were both driven in pushing the boundaries. They found the transitional state just before falling asleep to be highly conducive to radical ideas.

In fact, they both used very similar methods to make sure they woke up as soon as they fell asleep, so could record any ideas they had.

Edison would take a catnap in a chair, holding steel balls in his hands. As he drifted off to sleep, his grip would relax and the balls would drop, waking him up. He said his mind was flooded with images and more often than not he'd have a new idea to research.

Salvador Dali, would sit in his chair holding a key in his right hand and beneath it, an upside down metal plate. Once he fell asleep the key clanged onto the plate and woke him up. In his book *The 50 Secrets of Magic Craftsmanship* he describes the experience: " ... this fugitive moment when you had barely lost consciousness and during which you cannot be assured of having really slept is totally sufficient, inasmuch as not a second more is needed for your physical and psychic being to be revivified by just the necessary amount of repose."

But you don't need to go to these lengths, to experience this state between sleep and wakefulness. Try setting your alarm half an hour before you have to get up. Then when the alarm goes off, try not to fall back to sleep and try to doze. If you do fall asleep, you've always got the snooze alarm to wake you up.

Being half asleep is a great state for your mind to wander and for unconscious thoughts to bubble up; but the fact that your mind is so unfocused makes it a lot harder to remember the thoughts you have. So make sure you've got a pen and paper or your phone by your bed, so you can record any ideas you have.

" Being half asleep is a great state for your mind to wander and for unconscious thoughts to bubble up. "

42 Just Say It

"Examine what is said and not who speaks."
Arab proverb

Have you ever had the experience of explaining a problem to someone and before they even say anything, something clicks and you realize what the solution is? Communicating your problem out loud is actually a very powerful tool that can often help you understand what's needed without the person you're talking to saying anything.

The Nodding Teddy Bear

A few of the benefits of verbalizing your problem are that it:

1. Makes it clearer
By stating your problem out loud you are forced to mentally organize all the information you have regarding the problem. It also separates the problem from any emotional mental chatter about your ability, deadlines, anxiety of possible failure, etc.

2. Simplifies the problem
Assume the person you are explaining the problem to has little or no knowledge of the subject. This forces you to think about what the essence of the problem is and makes you explain it as simply and clearly as possible.

3. Helps you think about the problem, not the solution
Instead of spending all your energy focusing on what the solution is, you can focus purely on the problem. This takes the pressure away from looking for an answer. It can also help you in accessing different or overlooked information.

4. Uses more of your brain
Saying the problem out loud engages many more areas of the brain than merely thinking about it. This creates more chances of new connections being made. That's why it also works so much better than just imagining you're telling someone about the problem.

Rubber Ducking

I know "Rubber Ducking" sounds like some terrible new form of torture, but really it's just an inanimate version of the nodding teddy bear. Instead of telling your problem to a person, tell it to a rubber duck.

The concept is popular in the software development industry and is sometimes known as "rubber duck debugging". You have a rubber duck beside your computer and when you have a problem you can't solve you explain it to your rubber duck. And talking to a rubber duck really does have its benefits:

Rubber ducks don't:

- Say they're too busy and ask you to come back later.
- Interrupt you at a vital point and make you lose your flow.
- Have meetings to go to.
- Yawn.

But if you find the idea of talking to a rubber duck too embarrassing, you can always email it. Write the problem down in an email to the duck or to someone you know. Even though you're not going to send it, visualizing them reading it will help you to explain the problem as clearly and as simply as possible.

Talking someone – or something – through your problem can often be enough to help you find an answer. And whether it means talking to a nodding teddy bear or a rubber duck, it's a lot less embarrassing than telling your boss you can't crack it.

> ❝ **Talking someone – or something – through your problem can often be enough to help you find an answer.** ❞

43 Give It the Overnight Test

"Have you not noticed that, often, what was dark and perplexing to you the night before, is found to be perfectly solved the next morning?"

Alexander Graham Bell

I've already talked about the negative effects of not getting a good night's sleep in Brainhack 23 (Sleep Well), but what about the positive effects of getting a good night's sleep?

One of the most important things is that it's YOU sleeping. What I mean is your prefrontal cortex, the centre for what makes you, you. That your personality, your decisions, your social controls – is asleep. The night is when your unconscious really does have free rein. It can do its work without interference.

Obviously part of this is making sense of the day's events and filing them away in long-term memory. But also, if there are any problems on your mind, your unconscious will work on those. A problem can seem insurmountable when you go to bed, but then when you wake up, it doesn't seem so daunting.

> **❝ If there are any problems on your mind, your unconscious will work on those. ❞**

Here's the part of Alexander Graham Bell's quote that precedes the one at the top of the page: "I am a believer in unconscious cerebration. The brain is working all the time, though we do not know it. At night, it follows up what we think in the daytime. When I have worked a long time on one thing, I make it a point to bring all the facts regarding it together before I retire; and I have often been surprised at the results."

If your unconscious is aware that your conscious mind has been working hard on a problem, come the night, it will put its full processing power behind it. But as with the "light bulb moment" in the day, your conscious mind needs to have been working hard on the problem and you need to passionately require an answer to get your unconscious to work on it.

It's like the classic children's fairytale, *The Elves and the Shoemaker*, where the penniless shoemaker lays out his last piece of cloth and in the night the elves come and turn it into a beautiful pair of shoes.

Sometimes the solution to a problem, or at least the direction you need to take, will be revealed to you in the morning. Sometimes even in your dreams. Either way, always make sure you make a note of any thoughts you have as soon as you wake up, otherwise they may fade away.

If you can remember your dreams, then you can see the unconscious at work. And our dreams, even though we have no control over them, are very good at solving our problems. This is because when we're dreaming our minds are in the REM state, which has been found to be highly conducive to fluid reasoning and flexible thought.

Researchers tested participants' ability to solve anagrams when they were woken from REM (dream) sleep, compared with when they were woken from normal sleep. When people were woken from REM sleep, they proved 32% better at solving anagrams.

Here are a few examples of great ideas that have come from dreams:

Frankenstein

On a cold night in June of 1816, a group of friends gathered around a fire in a villa on Lake Geneva. The host was Lord Byron, accompanied by John Polidori, Percy Shelley and his girlfriend Mary Godwin, soon to be Mary Shelley. They entertained themselves by reading out ghost stories and Byron proposed a competition to write a ghost story of their own. Unable to think of a story, young Mary Godwin became anxious: "Have you thought of a story? I was asked each morning, and each morning I was forced to reply with a mortifying negative."

The idea didn't just come out of nowhere, she had been thinking about it for days until one night, she had the dream "that haunted her midnight pillow."

The Sewing Machine

Sometimes, the breakthrough idea can
be hidden in a dream. In 1845 Elias Howe, who
invented the sewing machine, said that he'd already had
the idea of a machine with a needle which would go through
a piece of cloth, but he couldn't figure out exactly how it would
work. In his dream, cannibals were preparing to cook him and they were
dancing around the fire waving their spears. Howe noticed at the head
of each spear there was a small hole through the spearhead. The up and
down motion of the spear and the hole near the head, stayed with him
when he woke. This gave him the idea of passing the thread through
the needle close to the point, not copying needles used in hand sewing
where the eye is at the other end.

Google PageRank

When Larry Page was a 22-year-old graduate student at Stanford he was
struck in the middle of the night with a vision. In it, he somehow managed
to download the entire Web and by examining the links between the
pages he saw the world's information in an entirely new way. What Page
wrote down that night became the basis for an algorithm. He called it
PageRank and used it to power a new Web search engine called BackRub.
PageRank was a success, the name BackRub wasn't.

Again, these ideas didn't come out of nowhere. All three had been
desperate to find solutions to their problems.

To Sleep, Perchance to Solve a Problem

There is a way to help your unconscious work for you: set it a challenge. It
might sound silly, but it does work. If you engage your mind in a task just
before you go to sleep – if not solved it will certainly seem a lot clearer
in the morning. Say, for instance, you are unhappy in your job and don't
know whether to leave or not. When you think about it in the day, your

conscious mind is beset with different opinions and emotions on the subject. It's like sitting around a table with twenty friends debating the subject. They all genuinely want to help, but all the different opinions just make it all a bit overwhelming.

If you set the problem for your unconscious to work on, it has got access to all the facts and relevant information and can calmly work through it.

1. First, before you go to bed, spend thirty minutes thinking in a relaxed way about the problem or issue.

2. Then when you get into bed, actually write down the problem and ask the question out loud to your unconscious. Also give it a deadline. Too much pressure creates stress; you don't want to be lying awake thinking about the problem. That will just be the problem going round and round in your conscious mind and won't be helping at all. But a little bit of gentle pressure can help, so set a time that you want the answer for. Using the example I mentioned earlier, say out loud and write down: "I am unhappy in my job and want to know what I should do. I would like an answer by 7:00 in the morning when I wake up."

3. When you wake up write down any immediate thoughts or insightful dreams you can remember. But don't worry if the answer doesn't seem obvious. Have a shower, which again can be a very productive place for unconscious ideas to bubble up.

4. Next make yourself a tea or coffee and sit down in a comfortable chair with a pen and a pad of paper. Now for half an hour just write. Don't think too much about what you're writing, or if it makes any sense. Just get your thoughts down on paper.

5. After you've read back what you've written, let the council of your conscious mind debate it.

You really will be surprised how much clearer things are after a good night's sleep.

44 Plan a Pre-Mortem

> "Criticism may not be agreeable, but it is necessary.
> It fulfils the same function as pain in the human body.
> It calls attention to an unhealthy state of things."
> *Winston Churchill*

There's a lot of talk these days about failing. Failing's good. Fail and fail fast. The idea, obviously, is that it's better to make mistakes early on and learn from them. But why not learn before you make the mistakes?

That's the idea behind the pre-mortem, created by Gary Klein, behavioural economist and psychologist, famous for his work in the field of naturalistic decision-making. It's very simple really. You imagine a time in the future after your business/project/idea has been launched. And in this imaginary future your idea has been a complete failure. "Unlike a typical critiquing session, in which project team members are asked what might go wrong, the pre-mortem operates on the assumption that the 'patient' has died."

Now you're probably thinking: Isn't this very negative? Aren't all these business successes started by people who are really positive go-getters who believe nothing is impossible and failure is not an option?

That's true to a degree, but also projects that are a success are also the ones that don't have any little chinks in their armour.

Only 50% of businesses survive the first five years. So it's important to make your idea as good and as strong as it can be.

Again this exercise isn't just for big projects like starting a new business; it could just be a presentation to a client, or even on a personal level like packing for a family holiday. In a way, how parents prepare for trips is a lot better than how many people launch their new projects in the business world. You see, parents are worriers; they imagine the worst. "What happens if it rains all the time" (British-specific holiday), "What happens if the children get hurt?" or "What happens if they find the journey too long?"

66 Projects that are a success are also the ones that don't have any little chinks in their armour. 99

Whereas a lot of business people would want everyone to be pumped up and positive about a project, already thinking about how they can scale it; parents think about what could go wrong.

And that's exactly the idea behind the pre-mortem. If you can imagine what could go wrong, you can fix it before it ever happens.

❝ If you can imagine what could go wrong, you can fix it before it ever happens. ❞

Now you might say, "Well, that's just planning, isn't it?" but it's actually a lot more effective than planning. When you're planning, you are imagining your project in the future, but you have a cognitive bias so you're imagining it as a success. When you're imagining the future of your project, you naturally want it to succeed, so you think of it in a positive light.

Accentuate the Negative

At Pixar they have an idea called "the Braintrust". In his book *Creativity, Inc.*, Ed Catmull tells how it started out with the five key men who led the production of *Toy Story*. It has since grown, but its one golden rule is: candour.

Ed says that in the beginning, all the Pixar films "suck". What the Braintrust does is discuss the current film in a completely honest and truthful way. There are no egos; everyone there is just trying to make the film as good as it can be. It also has no authority, so after each session the director and producer of the film are under no pressure to take on board any of the recommendations. However, they know it's far better to learn about problems from colleagues when there's still time to fix them than from the audience after it's too late.

I'm sure most companies would be happy to have the success that Pixar films have; but unfortunately not all companies are as open and egoless.

But even in an organization with big egos, the principles of Pixar's Braintrust can be recreated with the pre-mortem. Basically, it gives everyone permission to be negative.

Imagining your project was a complete failure has a magical effect. This is especially true in business when you have a group of people involved in the project. It removes the pressure from those who are worried about seeming disloyal by voicing concerns. It actually turns it into a competition to find the most convincing reason why the project should fail. "It's a sneaky way to get people to do contrarian, devil's-advocate thinking without encountering resistance", says Klein.

This "prospective hindsight" has actually been proven to work. Research by Mitchell, Russo and Pennington[1] has proved that imagining an event has already occurred, increases the ability to correctly identify reasons for future outcomes by 30%.

Academic Karl Weick argues that the reason it works is because of a cognitive quirk: we find it easier to imagine the detailed causes of a single outcome than causes of multiple outcomes.

By imagining the project has failed, it really helps us to focus. Instead of asking what could go wrong, you ask what did go wrong. There's a subtle difference that frees up your thinking and will create better results. Nobel prize winner Daniel Kahneman says, "The main virtue of the pre-mortem is that it legitimizes doubt".

Legitimized Bitching

The good thing with team members really pushing to find reasons why a project failed is they can discover quite obscure reasons that wouldn't have normally been thought about.

Here's an example that Gary Klein gives: In a session held at one Fortune 50–size company, an executive suggested that a billion-dollar environmental sustainability project had "failed" because interest waned when the CEO retired. Another pinned the failure on a dilution of the business case after a government agency revised its policies.

So how do you run a pre-mortem session?

1. Gather your team together and get them to imagine the project you've all been working so hard on, has been launched and has been a complete and utter failure.

2. Give everyone five minutes to write down any possible reason they can think of for this failure, especially the kinds of things they wouldn't normally mention for fear of being seen as overly negative or impolite.

3. Next, the session leader asks each member of the team to read one reason from his or her list. Everyone states a different reason until all of them have been recorded.

4. After the session the project manager or core team reviews the list.

5. A further meeting is held to look at the most likely problem areas and discuss ways to strengthen and improve the project.

And don't just believe because you've been really successful in the past, you will carry on being. You should always put every project under the microscope. That's what Pixar do with each of their films and that's why they are so successful.

Don't be wise after the event – be wise before it!

45 Make a Story of It

"We tell ourselves stories in order to live."
Joan Didion

"Now children, how about a nice bedtime PowerPoint?" said their father. Not something you're going to hear any time soon. Children would never sit through a PowerPoint presentation, so why do adults? Do we find it any more interesting? Of course not.

If you can bring a story to life for children, you'll have a rapt audience. But if you don't engage them they'll get bored and lose interest really quickly. Adults are no different; they're just more polite.

Death by Bullet Point

The obvious argument for PowerPoint is that a lot of presentations have a lot of information that needs to be communicated. But what's the point of having all this information if no one remembers it?

Jessica Lawrence of New York Tech Meetup had a problem. She and her colleague were struggling to communicate to a tech firm about what they wanted from their customer relationship management (CRM) system. There was a lot of information, but they wanted to make an interesting presentation.

> **What's the point of having all this information if no one remembers it?**

She needed a new way to communicate the idea that something was broken, something that had the potential to be much, much, better. So she opened a Word document and typed: "Once upon a time ...", then she finished the sentence: "there was a Girl Scout council with an amazing CRM system."

Lawrence went on to write an entire fairy tale, following several characters who work at a Girl Scout council that had a perfect CRM system that did everything she and her colleagues wanted. It was realistic about how people behaved, how software could fit into their lives.

She recalls, "I knew some people would find it incredibly weird, but I kind of didn't care. I was trying to solve a problem."

She then sent the fairy tale to the tech consultants. They loved it.

The reason story is so much more engaging is simple: it engages a lot more of our brain. Whether we're reading about an experience or encountering it in real life, it seems the same neurological regions are stimulated.

When we watch a PowerPoint presentation, it just activates a couple of parts of the brain: Broca's area and Wernicke's area. These are the areas of the brain that interpret written words. But what scientists have discovered is that narratives actually activate parts of the brain that relate to what is happening in the story, suggesting why the experience of reading can feel so alive. Words like "perfume", "cinnamon" and "coffee", for example, elicit a response not only from the language-processing areas of our brains, but also those devoted to dealing with smells.

66 The reason story is so much more engaging is simple: it engages a lot more of our brain. 99

Also if you can paint a picture in people's minds, whether written or spoken, it can have a powerful effect. A team of researchers from Emory University reported in *Brain and Language*[1] that when subjects in their laboratory read a metaphor involving texture, the sensory cortex, responsible for perceiving texture through touch, became active. Metaphors like "The singer had a velvet voice" and "He had leathery hands" roused the sensory cortex, while phrases matched for meaning, like "The singer had a pleasing voice" and "He had strong hands," did not. It was also found that figures of speech like "a rough day" are so familiar that they are treated simply as words and don't activate different areas of the brain like other less everyday metaphors.

John Bargh from Yale University and Lawrence Williams from the University of Colorado, ran a series of experiments to show how engrained metaphor is in how we think.

Volunteers would meet one of the experimenters, believing that they would be starting the experiment shortly. In reality, the experiment began when the experimenter, seemingly struggling with an armful of folders, asked the volunteer to briefly hold their coffee. As the key experimental manipulation, the coffee was either hot or iced. Subjects then read a description of some individual, and those who had held the warmer cup tended to rate the individual as having a warmer personality, even though there was no change in ratings of other attributes.

Bringing Life to a Story

The reason why stories have such an effect on us is that's how we're wired.

A good example of this is how we anthropomorphize things. It's our natural inclination to make a story out of things. A classic 1944 study by Fritz Heider and Mary-Ann Simmel, then at Smith College, Massachusetts, elegantly demonstrated this tendency. The psychologists showed people an animation of a pair of triangles and a circle moving around a square (trbq.org/play/) and asked the participants what was happening. The subjects described the scene as if the shapes had intentions and motivations; for example, "The circle is chasing the triangles." Many studies since then have confirmed the human predilection to make characters and narratives out of whatever we see in the world around us.

Another reason we're so attached to stories is we remember information better through story. Before the written word, huge amounts of information was passed down through generations by oral storytelling. Creating a story is the method World Memory Champion Ben Pridmore used to remember the order of a random deck of cards in 25 seconds. In his mind he placed the cards at certain points along a route familiar to him. Later when he walks the route in his mind he sees the cards one after another.

We live through stories. Every time we meet someone, we start to make a story up about him or her in our minds. Storytelling is so engrained in the human experience that personal stories and gossip make up 65% of conversation.

When we hear a story, we immediately try to relate it to one of our existing experiences. While we are busy searching for a similar experience in our brains, we activate a part of the brain called the insula, which helps us relate to that same experience of pain, joy, or disgust.

Because our brains are built for stories, they absorb them more readily than other kinds of information. Recent psychological studies suggest that people are more open to ideas when they're listening to stories than when they're listening to factual information.

> ## Because our brains are built for stories, they absorb them more readily than other kinds of information.

We don't just imagine stories: we experience them.

We don't just hear them: we feel them.

So if you've got an important message to get across to people that you want to resonate with them and be remembered, ditch the PowerPoint and tell a story.

The End.

YOUR BRAIN

100 BILLION NEURONS

100 TRILLION CONNECTIONS

AND YOU ONLY COMMAND 5% OF IT

NOW IT'S TIME TO TAKE BACK CONTROL

EVERY THOUGHT AND ACTION

REWIRES YOUR BRAIN

THINK AND ACT WISELY

BE CURIOUS

BE KIND

BE QUIET

EXERCISE YOUR BODY
EXERCISE YOUR MIND
THINK HARD
SLEEP
LAUGH
WRITE DON'T TYPE
GO FOR A WALK
DON'T FEAR THE BLANK PAGE
AND LEARN TO LOVE THE BLOCK
BE CONSCIOUS OF YOUR UNCONSCIOUS
LISTEN TO YOUR THOUGHTS
SHORT-CIRCUIT YOUR MIND'S SHORTCUTS

REFERENCES

1 Make a Done List

1 Jerry Seinfeld's Productivity Secret by Brad Isaac, *Lifehacker,* July 24, 2007, lifehacker.com/281626/jerry-seinfelds-productivity-secret

12 Don't Be Biased

1 Extraneous Factors in Judicial Decisions by S. Danziger, J. Levav and L. Avnaim-Pesso, *PNAS,* 108(17): 6889-6892, April 26, 2011, www.pnas.org/content/108/17/6889.full.pdf+html

2 Predicting Hunger: The Effects of Appetite and Delay on Choice by D. Read and B. van Leeuwen, *Organ Behav Hum Decis Process*, 76(2): 189-2015, Nov 1998, www.ncbi.nlm.nih.gov/pubmed/9831521

3 Bias Blind Spot: Structure, Measurement, and Consequences by I. Scopelliti, C.K. Morewedge, E. McCormick, H.L. Min, S. Lebrecht and K.S. Kassam, *Management Science,* 61(10): 2468-2486, 2015, pubsonline.informs.org/doi/abs/10.1287/mnsc.2014.2096

16 Make Fewer Decisions

1 Here's the Real Reason Mark Zuckerberg Wears the Same T-Shirt Every Day by E. Kim, Business Insider UK, Nov 7, 2014, uk.businessinsider.com/mark-zuckerberg-same-t-shirt-2014-11?r=US&IR=T

2 Why I Wear the Same Thing to Work Every Day by Matilda Kahl, Harpers Bazaar, Apr 3, 2015, www.harpersbazaar.com/culture/features/a10441/why-i-wear-the-same-thing-to-work-everday/

3 Creative Thinking: Why a Morning Routine Helps Conserve Your Brainpower by E. De Vita, ft.com, Feb 22, 2015, www.ft.com/cms/s/0/3d07fcea-b37b-11e4-9449-00144feab7de.html#axzz3tp9Oe4za

20 Just Start

1 Steel, P. (2007) The Nature of Procrastination. *Psychological Bulletin* (vol. 133 (1)) Jan 2007. 65-94

23 Sleep Well

1 Sleep-Deprived Brains Alternate Between Normal Activity and "Power Failure", *Society of Neuroscience*, May 20, 2008, www.sfn.org/Press-Room/News-Release-Archives/2008/Sleep-Deprived-Brains-Alternate-Between-Normal-Activity-and-Power-Failure

2 Ibid.

3 *Sleep Deprivation and Its Effects on Cognitive Performance,* by J. Dorrian and D.F. Dingles, John Wiley & Sons, Inc, 2005, onlinelibrary.wiley.com/doi/10.1002/0471751723.ch19/summary

4 Why Your Students (And You) Need Daytime Naps: How Napping Can Dramatically Improve Learning & Memory, by Saga Briggs, informED, Jun 27, 2015, www.opencolleges.edu.au/informed/features/napping-can-dramatically-improve-learning-memory/

25 Take Notes

I Watch Woody Allen Dip Into His Idea Drawer by M. Lyons, Vulture.com, Nov 16, 2011, www.vulture.com/2011/11/woody-allen-idea-drawer-american-master.html

29 Run a Brain Marathon

1 The Lessons I Learnt on an Entrepreneur's Island by S.A. Álvarez, virgin .com, Nov 24, 2014, www.virgin.com/entrepreneur/the-lessons-i-learnt-on-an-entrepreneurs-island

32 Think Like a Child

1 Do Schools Kill Creativity by K. Robinson, TED Talks, Feb 2006, www.ted .com/talks/ken_robinson_says_schools_kill_creativity?language=en

2 Why Our IQ Levels Are Higher Than Our Grandparents' by James Flynn, TED Talks, Sep 26, 2013, www.youtube.com/watch?v=9vpqilhW9uI

3 IBM 2010 Global CEO Study: Creativity Selected as Most Crucial Factor for Future Success, May 18, 2010, www-03.ibm.com/press/us/en/pressrelease/31670.wss

36 Work Messy

1 Physical Order Produces Healthy Choices, Generosity, and Conventionality, Whereas Disorder Produces Creativity by K. Vohs, J.P. Redden and R. Rahinel, *Psychological Science,* 24(9): 1860-1867, Sep 2013, pss.sagepub.com/content/24/9/1860

37 Enjoy Being Blocked

1 *A Guide for the Perplexed: Conversations with Paul Cronin* by Werner Herzog, Faber & Faber, 2014

44 Plan a Pre-Mortem

1 Back to the Future: Temporal Perspective in the Explanation of Events by D.J. Mitchell, J.E. Russo and N. Pennington, *Journal of Behaviorial Decision Making,* 2(1): 25-38, Jan/Mar, 1989, onlinelibrary.wiley.com/doi/10.1002/bdm.3960020103/abstract

45 Make a Story of It

1 Metaphorically Feeling: Comprehending Textural Metaphors Activates Somatosensory Cortex by S. Lacey, R. Stilla and K. Sathian, *Brain Lang,* 120(3): 416-421, Mar, www.ncbi.nlm.nih.gov/pubmed/22305051

IMAGE AND ILLUSTRATION CREDITS

pvi, vii, 4 Idea design – © Johavel/istockphoto.com

pvi, vii, 4 Bubbles for speech – © Ferdiperdozniy/istockphoto.com

pviii, ix, 100 Bulb idea – © Johavel/istockphoto.com

p2, 23 Brain – © Tortuga/shutterstock.com

p2 Bonsai – © Prodepran/istockphoto.com

p6 Happy businessman with checklist – © Antoniu/istockphoto.com

p8 Abstract 2015 calendar template – Kaca1 © /istockphoto.com

p15 Positive thinking – © Nuranvectorgirl/istockphoto.com

p16, 17 Human cells – © Ttsz/istockphoto.com

p21 Help – © Suat Gürsözlü/istockphoto.com

p23 Legs – © RamCreativ/istockphoto.com

p27 Musical notes – © Gun2becontinued/istockphoto.com

p34 Switch – © Vertyr/istockphoto.com

p41 Black cat in a bunny suit © Vivienstock/thinkstockphotos.co.uk

p49 Silhouette street violinist – © Aarrows/istockphoto.com

p51 Savings – © Nousha/istockphoto.com

p55 Man with loudspeaker – © Puruan/istockphoto.com

p56 Businessman debt – © Wissanu99/istockphoto.com

p58 Businessman listening to music – © Jack191/istockphoto.com

p59 Pudding jelly – © Yitewang/istockphoto.com

p63 Arrow background – © Mattjeacock/istockphoto.com

p65 Calendar – © Dacian_G/istockphoto.com

p65 Stopwatch – © Gheatza/istockphoto.com

p68 Notepad and pen – © Gmast3r/istockphoto.com

p81 Question mark created from cog wheels – © Muuraa/istockphoto.com

p90 Ballpoint pen – © Vtis/istockphoto.com

p92 Light bulb with long wire – © Owat Tasai/istockphoto.com

p95 Boiled egg – © SimonDGCrinks/istockphoto.com

p98 Creativity – © Erhui1979/istockphoto.com

p98 Pen – © Anthonycz/istockphoto.com

p102, 103 Vector arrows © -Slav-/istockphoto.com

p106 Marathon banner – © Pialhovik/istockphoto.com

p111 Think different – © Mack2happy/istockphoto.com

p113 Brain and cloud – © Dr911/istockphoto.com

p115 Puzzle design – © Jemastock/istockphoto.com

p122, 123 Scribble black bubbles – © Artishokcs/istockphoto.com

p134 Breaking the wall – © Ojogabonitoo/istockphoto.com

p144 Ajar door light beam concept – © ChrisGorgio/istockphoto.com

p145 Blank Rubik's cube – © ARTWatcharapong/istockphoto.com

p146 Grunge white and black brick wall – © Angel_1978/istockphoto.com

p148 Colorful footprints border – © FreeSoulProduction/istockphoto.com

p150 Slide to unlock icon – © Furtaev/istockphoto.com

p153 Person daydreaming – © Noedelhap/istockphoto.com

p155 Good night – © Cotyledons/istockphoto.com

p157 Business man dreaming – © iNueng/istockphoto.com

p159 Rubber duck – © Richardburditt/istockphoto.com

p167 Time is money – © Liravega/istockphoto.com

p170 Book story with child and tree – © Locotearts/istockphoto.com

p170 Summer tree – © Kudryashka/istockphoto.com

Illustrations by Curtis Allen: p13, 25, 30, 39, 47, 61, 89, 109, 125, 129, 141

All other visuals and page design by Andy Prior Design Ltd

ABOUT THE AUTHOR

Neil Pavitt is a writer and creativity coach. He is passionate about helping people discover and realize their own creative potential.

On the quest to reach his own creative potential he has written a book demystifying the creative process called *How To Be Creative*. He has been a writer in advertising and television and won many prestigious awards in these industries. He has also had a short film nominated for the BAFTA New Writers award and spent a stint as a stand-up comedian.

As well as writing, he currently runs workshops on creativity, brainhacking and brand storytelling.

For more information go to www.thelightbulbidea.com or email him at neil@thelightbulbidea.com

ACKNOWLEDGEMENTS

Firstly I'd like to thank my wife Kalya for all her help in making this book happen, and also my son Harry for putting up with me working through nearly all of his summer holidays.

I'd like to thank my mum for all her support and encouragement. My brothers Andrew and James as well as Craig Storti, Roy Millman and Jane Simmons for their thoughts and feedback.

I'd also like to thank Holly, Jenny, Vicky, Sam, Emma and everyone else at Capstone for making this book a reality.

Finally in addition to all the neuroscientists and psychologists whose experiments and ideas made this possible; I'd like to thank all the websites, writers and bloggers who've brought them to my attention:

Daniel Kahneman, Gary Klein, Maria Konnikova, David Eagleman, Adam Atler, Julia Cameron, Oliver Burkeman, Dan Ariely, Maria Popova and brainpickings.com, Eric Barker, Shane Parrish, Belle Beth Cooper, Elizabeth Segran, *Harvard Business Review, New Yorker, Wired, Time Magazine, Fast Company,* TED, *New York Times,* inc.com, 99u.com by Behance, *The Huffington Post, The Atlantic, Scientific American Mind* and *New Scientist.*

NOTES